ALSO BY CHRIS MATTHEWS

Now, Let Me Tell You What I Really Think

Hardball

Kennedy & Nixon

AMERICAN

Beyond Our Grandest Notions

CHRIS MATTHEWS

Free Press
New York London Toronto Sydney Singapore

FREE PRESS
A Division of Simon & Schuster, Inc.
1230 Avenue of the Americas
New York, NY 10020

Copyright © 2002 by Christopher Matthews
All rights reserved,
including the right of reproduction
in whole or in part in any form.

First Free Press trade paperback edition 2003

FREE PRESS and colophon are trademarks
of Simon & Schuster, Inc.

For information about special discounts for bulk purchases,
please contact Simon & Schuster Special Sales:
1-800-456-6798 or business@simonandschuster.com

Manufactured in the United States of America

1   3   5   7   9   10   8   6   4   2

The Library of Congress has catalogued the hardcover edition as follows:

Matthews, Christopher, 1945–
American: beyond our grandest notions/Chris Matthews.
p. cm.
Includes bibliographical references (p.) and index.
1. National characteristics, American. 2. United States—Civilization.
I. Title.

E169.1 .M429 2002
973'.099—dc21   2002034741

ISBN 0-7432-4086-3
ISBN 0-7432-4087-1 (Pbk)

To Michael, Thomas, and Caroline

Contents

ACKNOWLEDGMENTS

On the last, unforgettable page of *The Great Gatsby*, F. Scott Fitzgerald wrote of the New World as the early sailors must have first glimpsed it. "For a transitory enchanted moment man must have held his breath in the presence of this continent . . . face to face for the last time in history with something commensurate to his capacity for wonder."

In writing this tribute to the grand notions that enchant this country, it's been my fortune and joy to rediscover that wonder.

For this I want to thank my beautiful wife Kathleen. She knew the challenges of this wide-ranging project and how to meet them. It was her generous and strategic counsel that made this book possible.

I want to thank my dad for getting me excited about the movies and my high school English teacher Gerald Tremblay for getting me excited about literature.

I want to thank my editor Dominick Anfuso for his leadership and friendship in once again turning an exciting concept into reality; also his assistant Wylie O'Sullivan and my other friends at Free Press: Martha Levin, Carolyn Reidy, Michele

Jacob, Alexandra Fox, Edith Lewis, Nancy Inglis, Paul Dippolito, and Beth Maglione.

I want to thank my brilliant researcher Richard Lee. To paraphrase the slogan of the Royal Canadian Mounted Police, he always gets the goods.

Whether it was a scene from a movie, a line from a novel, a relevant work of criticism or an episode from history, my relentless colleague tracked it down. Rich advised and counseled me from the start. Without him, this project could not have been undertaken, much less completed.

Ben Simmoneau, my second researcher, was my other wise and energetic partner. His fine intelligence was critical at the project's beginning, decisive in its final weeks. He was ably assisted by Inez Russo, also by Julia Bain, Lindsay Jaffee, Meghan Dwyer, and Kristen Thorne.

I want to thank Michele Slung, once again, for her brilliant editing and counsel. You are indeed a friend when *I* am in need. I want to thank my assistant Meaghan Nolan for her excellent coordination of the project. As always, I am indebted to my loyal, audacious literary agent Raphael Sagalyn, who encouraged my book writing career from the outset.

I want to thank Nancy Morrissey of U.S. Congressman Edward Markey's office for her help with the Library of Congress, also Nancy Ives and Rebecca Hanks of Senator John McCain's office. Special thanks to Tim Dirks and www.filmsite.org for his contribution to my movie research.

Acknowledgments

From MSNBC's *Hardball,* I want to thank my Washington colleagues Dominic Bellone, David Schuster, Christina Jamison, Howard Mortman, and Kerri Forrest. For his dynamic leadership, I thank *Hardball* executive producer Philip Griffin, also senior producer Noah Oppenheim and my *Hardball* colleagues at MSNBC headquarters: Rani Brand, Court Harson, Mike Tirone, Rick Jefferson, Jeff Wynnyk, E. J. Johnson, Beck Schoenfeld, Jessica Jensen, and Falguni Lakhani.

My special thanks, of course, to NBC chairman Robert C. Wright, NBC president Andrew Lack, NBC News president Neal Shapiro, and MSNBC president Erik Sorensen.

Finally, I want to thank Richard Leibner for representing me so extraordinarily well in my television work. His professionalism, loyalty, and moxie are in a class by themselves.

American

Prologue

France was a land, England was a people, but America, having about it still that quality of the idea, was harder to utter—it was the graves at Shiloh and the tired, drawn, nervous faces of its great men, and the country boys dying in the Argonne for a phrase that was empty before their bodies withered. It was a willingness of the heart.

F. SCOTT FITZGERALD

This is one man's look at his country. It's also a look at America the way we *Americans* want to be looked at.

For me, it has been a journey of rediscovery, an often nostalgic trip back through the books and movies of my youth and those heroes whom I've never forgotten. It was thrilling to learn that what worked for me then works for me now.

The journey took me further than I expected, back to the very beginning of this country. In uncovering the kinship between my literary and cinematic upbringing and the heroic history of my country, I was struck by the potency of our shared *American-ness*.

Talk about power. What stirred the souls of our ancestors two centuries ago—and through all the generations in between—still does.

Our cowboy love of freedom is a prime example. While it can mean different things to different people, it's at the center of everything we Americans care about.

But there's a lot more to being—and feeling—American than that. And now's a damn good time to say what it is.

For myself, the answer to the question of just who we *are* can be found in the great American romance we have been celebrating for over two hundred years. What I mean by that is the picture of America and Americans that grabs at even the toughest heart. The best part of writing this book was revisiting that romance. I went back to my favorite characters—from Shane to Jay Gatsby to Humphrey Bogart in *Casablanca*. I saw that they are part of something bigger, anchored in our unique history, present even now in our contemporary politics.

What else did I learn?

That being an American means buying into some very distinct notions.

Start with our view of war. Remember the airport scene in *Casablanca* when Bogie gives up the girl he loves? He does it because he recognizes that even his desire for the beautiful Ilsa doesn't "amount to a hill of beans" in the face of the ascendant Nazi evil. A stateless man of the world, he turns patriot once the stakes are clear.

George Washington would have understood. To the great general of the American Revolution, military action was a "last resort" and nothing more. War should be the *exception* to American life. He warned in his farewell address to avoid "permanent alliances" that would drag us into other conflicts. "I want an American character that the powers of Europe may be convinced we act for ourselves and not for others," he told his friend Patrick Henry.

In today's world Secretary of State Colin Powell, himself a former general, champions the same view. Like George Washington, he would be at home in Rick's Café Americain. "War should be the politics of last resort," he has written—and I believe he means it.

Our resistance to foreign entanglements is matched by our resistance to big government. It should be no surprise that the most beloved American political movie, Frank Capra's *Mr. Smith Goes to Washington,* is about rot at the top.

Something of a scandal in itself when it opened in 1939, it showed the men running things in Washington as moral eunuchs. Angry senators stormed out of the premiere at Constitution Hall. The politically influential Joseph P. Kennedy, father of the future president, was so outraged that he demanded it be yanked from theaters.

This fable of youthful idealism triumphing over aging cynicism perfectly captures America's mistrust of the ruling elite. We cheer for the gallant young Jefferson Smith, who refuses to be licked even when the entire establishment lines up to destroy him. It was his namesake, Thomas Jefferson, after all, who counseled that "a little rebellion now and then" was good for the country.

The spirit of the rebellious Mr. Smith lives on in the same way as does the reluctant fighter of Bogie's Rick Blaine. If Secretary Powell can be considered the avatar of Bogie and George Washington, Senator John McCain is the embodiment of the democratic pugnacity that fueled the indignation of Jimmy Stewart's Mr. Smith. As a defiant POW in North Vietnam, McCain stood up to his captors. As a U.S. senator, he has fought the corrupt role of money in politics with the same indignation as the celluloid Smith, once stirred to action, did.

There are other distinctly American notions:

- We have this peculiar penchant for enshrining misfits as heroes. Think of the driven Ethan Edwards, as played by a demonic John Wayne, in *The Searchers* or that obsessed loner, Robert De Niro's Travis Bickel in *Taxi Driver*. We love heroes who wouldn't fit in unless they were heroes. Could this be because we as a country don't quite fit with other countries?

- Americans are a self-invented people. Here any person has a right to try and become who he or she wants to be. This could explain why *The Great Gatsby* retains its hold on our collective imagination. Even as it cautions against the grown-up dangers of acting out a youthful fantasy, it enshrines the lure that brings millions of people to this country ready to learn English, change their names, and grab for the brass ring.

- We Americans love people who have proved themselves in action. This goes for writers as well as presidents. Ernest Hemingway is the Great American Writer—but not just because of the books he turned out. He was larger than life, certainly larger than anyone else sitting behind a typewriter. He was shot as an ambulance driver on the Italian front in World War I, ran with the bulls in Spain, and hunted big game in East Africa. By force of his life's example, he took the writer's life out of the garret and placed it against a panorama of high adventure.

- Americans cherish the idea that any regular person can rise even to the country's highest office, if they have the right stuff. Three of our most legendary presidents, Andrew Jackson, Abraham Lincoln, and Harry Truman, had practically no formal schooling. They were common men of uncommon ability, and that was what counts.

- Americans root for the underdog. Oprah Winfrey is a media colossus for a reason. She does more than empathize with wounded people trying to heal themselves. She is someone who was hurt herself but refused to quit. This same unwillingness to stay down is what made *Rocky* a movie that had audiences applauding with tears in their eyes.

- We are a country that will not abandon its pioneer past. The American frontier may be gone but its spirit lives on. From Daniel Boone in the Kentucky wilderness to Charles Lindbergh soaring high and alone above the choppy Atlantic to John F. Kennedy and his daring call to shoot for the moon, we Americans don't like to get anywhere second.

- We are also a country of unabashed optimism. Even our critics see in us a confidence about our future that sets us apart and that has a way of being self-fulfilling. In what were some of our darkest times—battling a huge economic crisis at home or military foes overseas—Franklin Roosevelt understood the thirst the American people have for optimism. "This great nation will endure as it has endured," he said with perfect confidence that first day from the Capitol steps, "will revive and will prosper." FDR was handsomely rewarded for his optimism with an unprecedented four terms as president.

- Finally, we Americans see ourselves endowed with a special destiny. Even before the Puritans reached landfall, John Winthrop spoke of building a "city upon a hill," a role model for all the world. Thomas Paine saw the American Revolution as a break not just with Europe but with the past. "We have it in our power to begin the world all over," he wrote.

I write this book uplifted by the *fact* that America has outdone the grandest notions of its founders. Yet I worry that we might unknowingly forfeit this legacy of who we are.

I hope, as you read these chapters, you will grasp the stakes. We Americans learn early these notions from our shared past. If we're lucky, they never leave us. They are what make us and our country great. The purpose of this book is to remind us of that single splendid fact.

CHAPTER 1

A Self-Made Country

The GREAT GATSBY

F·SCOTT·FITZGERALD

> The truth was that Jay Gatsby of West Egg, Long Island sprang from his Platonic conception of himself.
>
> F. SCOTT FITZGERALD, *THE GREAT GATSBY*

There was once an upscale men's shop in the Georgetown section of Washington, D.C., that featured a shiny metal nameplate over the door of its dressing room. It noted that the shop had been honored to have had among its patrons Mr. Cary Grant. It seemed that the gentleman had experienced some unusually warm weather during a visit to Washington and needed a lighter weight suit than he'd brought along. It concluded the historic note by saying Mr. Grant had used this very same changing room to try on his unexpected purchase.

Why would a relatively posh men's store in a high-end neighborhood make such a big deal out of a movie star stripping down to his underwear on its premises? Why would a store serving the well-to-do and the sophisticated get so wobbly in the knees as to give this guy the "George Washington Slept Here" treatment?

The best answer is to see one of his movies.

In a whole string of roles from *Topper, Bringing Up Baby, Holiday,* and *Gunga Din* in the 1930s to *His Girl Friday, The Philadelphia Story,* and *Notorious* in the 1940s to *To Catch a Thief, An Affair to Remember,* and *North by Northwest* in the 1950s, Cary Grant was the very model of the debonair American gentleman. He was both democratic and aristocratic, a man so charming and self-assured that every woman wanted him, every man wanted to be like him. He was an acrobat in a business suit, a man of dignity with the subtle physicality of a clown, a regular guy knowing full well how fortunate he was to be wearing such an expensive, well-tailored suit.

"Do you know what's wrong with you?" one of his screen partners had pretended to scold him. "Nothing." Director Alfred Hitchcock dared to say, "Cary's the only thing I ever loved in my whole life."

As a matter of fact, the man we know as Cary Grant loved the idea of becoming this world-class charmer so much that he decided early in his adulthood to do it. Born in Bristol, England, in 1904, Archibald Alexander Leach was the son of a tailor's presser. How he got from there to having his nameplate on a Georgetown men's shop is a great American story.

He began as a working-class English kid doing pantomimes at the theater. Then he got himself into music hall acts mimicking the popular singers of the day. He later picked up some magic tricks. The praise he was denied at home he earned at the theater. Stagestruck, he came to America. Here he picked up odd jobs, earning five dollars a day, ten dollars on Saturday and Sunday, as a stilt-walker on Coney Island.

By 1931, Archie Leach was what he wanted to be—a working American actor. Landing the part of Cary Lockwood in a Broadway play, he liked the character's first name and decided to take it. He added "Grant" to make him sound more American.

Watching the great playwright-actor Noël Coward in *Private Lives* he decided to be Coward.

To achieve this transformation, he spent endless hours practicing how Coward walked, how he spoke, even his facial expressions. "I pretended to be somebody I wanted to be and I finally became that person," he would confess years later. "Or he became me. Or we met at some point."

At the age of twenty-seven, the man we would love as Cary Grant was born.

It wasn't as easy as it appeared. "I cultivated raising one eyebrow, and tried to imitate those who put their hands in their pockets with a certain amount of ease and nonchalance. But at times, when I put my hand in my trouser with what I imagined was great elegance, I couldn't get the blinking thing out again because it dripped from nervous perspiration."

What won Grant special devotion, however, was his refusal to deny who he was born. When we in the audience forgot about his background, he would remind us. "Listen!" he erupted in *His Girl Friday,* "the last man who said that to me was Archie Leach just a week before his throat was cut."

"It was a knowing wink to the audience, his audience, a secret shared with strangers," Grant's biographer Graham McCann noticed. "It was the kind of gesture that would have endeared someone like Cary Grant to someone like Archie Leach. Cary Grant was not conceived of as the contradiction of Archie Leach but as the constitution of his desires."

We couldn't imagine him ever dying, of course. This was especially true as he aged gracefully, giving up films to become an executive with Fabergé. "I don't know how I consider death," he said. "So many of my friends have been doing it recently. My only fear is that I don't embarrass others."

He didn't. Grant died at eighty-two during rehearsal for a touring one-man show featuring his old movie clips. "Everybody wants to be Cary Grant," the actor once admitted amid all the fawning. "Even I want to be Cary Grant."

Much like this beloved matinee idol, America itself is a confection. In the years after the Revolution, the Founding

Fathers had a vision of a country and government they wanted. They then very consciously, not unlike Archie Leach, turned that vision into reality.

Confecting a Capital

On a June afternoon in 1791, two gentlemen on horseback looked down from Jenkin's Hill onto a stretch of Maryland flatland banking the Potomac River. One, an architect, had designed a new national capital for this spot. The other, a trained surveyor, was the new government's first president.

Both Pierre L'Enfant and George Washington were men of vision and optimism. They had settled on a grand plan indeed: a capital city fit not for what had been just thirteen seaboard colonies but for a vast continental power. Jenkin's Hill, which L'Enfant called a "pedestal waiting for a monument," would one day be called Capitol Hill. L'Enfant's blueprints would become the world capital bearing the name of his companion on horseback that day.

When you think about it, this country designed itself. Just as L'Enfant and Washington built a capital from scratch, so did Thomas Jefferson and James Madison and the others design a new kind of government on a blank page. And if it seemed precocious for a French-born architect who'd never before done anything like it to design a national capital, it was more precocious still for a group of men who had never done anything like it before to confect a country, to guarantee as "unalienable" a set of rights the world had never before recognized, to ensure not only its citizens' lives and liberty but also their right to pursue "happiness."

And just as Washington and L'Enfant set wide bounds for the future growth of the new capital's geography, the designers of the Constitution generously conceived the new nation's freedoms. Americans could decide who they wanted to be and try to become it. A country that had dared design itself based on its own grandest notions would not stand in the way of its citizens harboring and pursuing their own grand notions. America would be a place where a person could be who he or she wanted to be.

And it was to be a place were people thought big.

If L'Enfant could choose a "monumental concept, with a capitol building and a 'president's house' " connected by a grand "public walk" to serve as the national seat for thirteen recently united colonies, then the American people could dare to be equally monumental in charting the contours and heights of their own lives.

Just as this new republic would, in Thomas Paine's words, "begin the world over again," it would certainly be a spacious and adventurous home to those hoping to do that with their own lives and ambitions. America would be a country where anyone could grab a second chance.

Here, the way things are is not the way they have to be. They can be the way individual Americans want them to be.

The Great Gatsby

In a country open to such big notions, the popularity of F. Scott Fitzgerald's *The Great Gatsby* should be no surprise. It's the story of Jay Gatsby, a young soldier training for World War I who meets a beautiful young socialite named Daisy. He falls in love with her only to get a letter while he is serving in the trenches of France, telling him that she has married Tom Buchanan, a wealthy young man from Yale. At a practical level, he'd known it was coming. Rich girls like Daisy didn't marry poor boys like him.

An eternal romantic, our hero refused to accept the verdict. Back from the war, Gatsby makes the right connections and becomes a rich bootlegger. Whatever it takes to become the man Daisy Buchanan would marry, he is prepared to do.

Having enriched himself beyond his wildest dreams, Jay Gatsby now sets about pursuing the only happiness he knows. He buys a giant mansion on Long Island right across the bay from the home of Daisy and Tom Buchanan. From there he maps plans to win her back. He hosts loud and lavish parties open to all in the hope that she will show up at one. Finally, he makes the acquaintance and seeks the aid of his neighbor. Nick Carraway, who he discovers is Daisy's cousin.

Carraway, the story's narrator, doesn't know what to make of the man presiding over the garish mansion next door. "I would have accepted without question the information that Gatsby sprang from the swamps of Louisiana or from the Lower East Side of New York. That was comprehensible. But young men didn't—at least in my provincial inexperience I believe they didn't—drift coolly out of nowhere and buy a palace on Long Island Sound."

But Gatsby needed more than money: he needed to be someone who had *always* had it.

"I'll tell you God's truth," he says to the skeptical Carraway. "I'm the son of some wealthy people in the middlewest—all dead now. I was brought up in America but educated at Oxford because all my ancestors have been educated there for many years. It is a family tradition."

For Jay Gatsby, the dream Daisy inspired in him is as important as the woman herself. It isn't what she felt, but what *he* felt.

"I wouldn't ask too much of her," Nick warns him. "You can't repeat the past."

"You can't repeat the past?" retorts an incredulous Gatsby. "Why of course you can!"

And: "I'm going to fix everything just the way it was before. . . . She'll see."

This blind faith that he can retrofit his very existence to Daisy's specifications is the heart and soul of *The Great Gatsby*. It's the classic story of the fresh start, the second chance.

"The truth was that Jay Gatsby of West Egg, Long Island, sprang from his Platonic conception of himself," Fitzgerald wrote. "He was the son of God—a phrase which, if it means anything, means just that—and he must be about His Father's Business, the service of a vast, vulgar, meretricious beauty. So he invented just the sort of Jay Gatsby that a seventeen year old boy would be likely to invent, and to this conception he was faithful to the end."

There was also Gatsby's smile. "It was one of those rare smiles with a quality of eternal reassurance in it, that you may come across four or five times in life. It faced—or seemed to face—the whole external world for an instant, and then concentrated on *you* with an irresistible prejudice in your favor. It understood you just so far as you wanted to be understood, believed in you as you would like to believe in yourself and assured you that it had precisely the impression of you that, at your best, you hoped to convey."

The reader, like Nick Carraway, comes to like this guy. We love his dream because we have, all of us, shared something very much like it. "Gatsby was not a character," said the critic Alfred Kazin, "but an idea of the everlasting self-creation that Americans have mastered."

Gatsby, for me, is undeniably the great American novel. We celebrate its hero and his "heightened sensitivity to the promises of life," his "extraordinary gift for hope," his "romantic readiness," because we as a country share every bit of it.

Grace Kelly

People think of Grace Kelly, the actress who became a European princess, as someone born to the role. In reality, Grace Patricia Kelly of East Falls, Philadelphia, was never a debutante, never applied for admission nor was received in Main Line society. She was a Roman Catholic and newly rich, a double bar to the ultra-restrictive social registry of that day.

But while she was never invited to make her debut by the Philadelphia Assemblies, she did possess an early claim to prominence: her father was a wealthy building contractor: "Kelly for Brickwork" was a familiar sign at area job sites.

John B. "Jack" Kelly was also a famous sculler in a city that to this day attaches great importance to the rowing sports. Yet he had become famous in his hometown as much for a notorious rejection as for his achievements. In 1919, Grace's dad was scratched as an entry in the Diamond Sculls at England's Henley Royal Regatta on the grounds that he had performed manual labor—that is, he had worked with

his hands. He was not, according to the Regatta's encrusted code, a gentleman.

Kelly reared his only son and namesake to one day avenge the slight. Grace, his second daughter, got no such paternal attention.

When she gained admission to New York's American Academy of Dramatic Arts in September of 1947, her dad was supremely unimpressed.

That would change.

Grace Kelly's ambition was to be the greatest Hollywood movie star ever. Two factors in her makeup made that a credible goal: the blond German beauty of her mother, combined with the Irish drive of her father.

However, the first sacrifice required of her was a daunting one. It was the way she talked: that grating Philly accent had to go. She could never be a big star with the sound of the rowhouses in her voice. She either had to lose it or give up on her dream.

"You have got to get rid of that terrible *twang*!" an Academy tutor would tell her point-blank. And so she did. For this, the American Academy of Dramatic Arts was perfectly suited. "It takes a trained ear to detect all errors of pronunciation, accent and emphasis," its brochure advertised, "but by careful and persistent criticism, the dialects of Pennsylvania or New England, of Canada or the South, are at last dethroned."

"When Grace Kelly pronounced the word 'rotten' you could hear every single 't' and a few more beside," biographer Robert Lacey reports, "while her vowel sounds, tugged firmly away from East Falls, had ventured out across the Atlantic to hover remarkably close to the British coast."

Grace no longer talked like her father, her mother, her brother or her sisters. To make her voice deeper and more resonant still, she would spend hours talking with a clothespin clasped to the end of her nose.

Her family was merciless. They called it "Gracie's new voice." A friend, hearing her at a cocktail party, decided she was actually speaking in a "British accent." Grace defended herself, saying frostily, "I must talk this way for my work."

"She got away from home early," her brother, Jack Kelly, Jr., agreed in admiration. "None of the rest of us managed to do that."

Her legendary film roles included *High Noon* with Gary Cooper; *Mogambo* with Clark Gable, for which she won an Oscar nomination for Best Supporting Actress; *Dial M for Murder* with Ray Milland; *Rear Window* with Jimmy Stewart; *The Country Girl* with Bing Crosby, for which she won the Oscar for Best Actress; and *To Catch a Thief* with Cary Grant, which brought her to the principality of Monaco and her final role.

It was when she came home to East Falls with that Academy Award for Best Actress—a certified movie queen—that she and her father experienced what I can only call a "Gatsby" moment. More than being simply her father's daughter, Grace Kelly now was greater than that. Her stardom made her the child of her own ambition. For the first time, the self-made, self-satisfied John B. Kelly had to accept that his offspring was daughter to a greater dream than his own.

This daughter, to whom he had given the least attention, the one in whom he had invested the least, the one who shared least in his love and devotion to athletic achievement, was now "Grace Kelly."

The joining of her aristocratic manner—so assiduously honed at acting school—to her American ambition was what it took to put the icing on the cake. Grace Kelly was about to become Her Serene Highness, Princess Grace of Monaco. Her tabloid-glamorous marriage to Prince Rainier elevated her even above her role as an American star. A queen of the silver screen, she was now the genuine article. When she died in a car crash in 1982, she was mourned as a royal. Her memory is cherished not least in our shared hometown, Philadelphia.

Ralph Lauren

The acronym WASP, for white Anglo-Saxon Protestant, was coined by Professor Digby Baltzell to describe the typical member of Philadelphia's Main Line society. Its allure arises as much from its exclusivity as from any inherent charm. But let's face it, it *sells*—cars, clothes, furniture, dreams.

Just check the latest edition of *Vanity Fair.*

"My look is not really European," Ralph Lauren has said. "It's an American's visualization of Europe in the 1930s. I look in from the other side." We can see in the faces in his Polo ads that easy arrogance that says "I was born to this." Just as Daisy Buchanan's voice carried the sound of money, Ralph Lauren's designs would give his customers the look of money.

But Lauren's true "other side" is Ralph Lifshitz, the ambitious designer son of Russian Jewish immigrants. The tanned, handsome man recognizable everywhere from the gorgeously patrician layouts selling his clothing and cosmetics started out as a Bronx salesman of gloves, ties, and perfume.

Lauren's big break came when in 1967 he managed to convince a leading neckwear company to carry a line of neckties that he had designed. The ties, constructed from leftover fabrics found in warehouses, were wider than the narrow ties fashionable in those years. Americans loved them, and an empire was born.

Say this for Ralph. He knew what we wanted because he was *us*. Growing up, young Lifshitz—just as we did—fell for screen stars Cary Grant, Humphrey Bogart, and Katharine Hepburn, attracted to their grand sense of style. And it's precisely their classic American aesthetic he's spent his life marketing. It didn't surprise me to learn that the staples of his line aren't so very different from the costumes he designed for the 1974 remake of *The Great Gatsby*.

The writer Neal Gabler argues that Lauren's popularity comes from knowing that Americans will "pay to transform their lives into their cinematic fantasies: safari outfits to make one a colonialist from *Out of Africa*; denim jackets and jeans to make one a cowboy from a Hollywood western; finely tailored English suits to make one an aristocrat from any number of crisp drawing room melodramas."

Lauren's flagship store on upper Madison Avenue, once a stately mansion, is the temple of assimilation where the newly rich come to worship the old rich and leave carrying clothes and furnishings that promise not just a comfortable look but a comforting history.

Lauren's furniture is "cunningly cinematic," writes Lauren-watcher Elizabeth Grice. "Long Island beaches, log cabins, English country houses, garden parties, the African bush. He dressed houses the way he dressed people, always mindful of the yearning for romance and escape . . . and the seductiveness of ideas."

The great seduction of America, he was not the first to notice, is that wildest of personal liberties: to be who you want to be.

A Self-Made People

To understand Americans, start with the fact that we're a self-made country.

It's an important notion. Free people gathered, articulated a social philosophy, designed a government and approved blueprints for a capital. Able to choose between British rule and self-government, they chose the latter, then defended the decision by force of arms. They discarded the society of their birth and constructed a new society of their choice. Had there not been an American Revolution, a Declaration of Independence, and a Constitution—all freely agreed to—there would not be a United States of America.

This was not the case for the British or the Germans or any other nationality from which we descended. Some of these evolved through tribe, treaty, and war, which was the pattern in Europe and Asia; others were carved up by imperial fiat, the norm in much of Africa and Latin America.

Many Americans would also create themselves *personally*.

Here a man or woman could change names, assume a new identity, hang out with other people who'd done likewise. It is the rare old acquaintance, much less a new one, who would question you seriously about your lineage or even ask casually what your father did for a living.

Such indifference to family and background leaves doors open here in socially mobile America that would be sealed shut in other, older, more regimented societies. Had Archie Leach stayed home in Bristol, England, Cary Grant would never have been born. Were this not America, a country where such things are possible, Grace Patricia Kelly would not have become a princess.

This freedom wasn't *given* to America. Rather, we grabbed it, held it, made it part of our Constitution. It shines today as our greatest national treasure. This country wasn't here when we got here. If we are as wise as we've been fortunate, that's something we'll never forget.

CHAPTER 2

The Constant Rebel

> I hold it that a little rebellion now and then is a good thing and as necessary in the political world as storms in the physical.
>
> THOMAS JEFFERSON

Ask a group of U.S. senators if there was a movie that gripped them with the romance of politics. Most, I know for a fact, will say *Mr. Smith Goes to Washington.*

Their choosing it makes for an extraordinary tribute to Frank Capra's 1939 classic—which came out in the early weeks of World War II—because it in fact casts a harsh light on the political world. We follow young Jefferson Smith from an unknown western state—presumably Montana—to a Washington that gets airbrushed from the civics books.

This Mr. Smith, who is enshrined in American legend—almost as if he were a hero of folklore—is an idealistic young man who finds himself picked to replace a U.S. senator who has died before completing his term. But Jeff Smith quickly discovers that he's a stooge put there by the state's corrupt political machine. He's been plucked from his troop of Boy Rangers to keep the seat warm and make no trouble.

Soon after his swearing-in, however, Jefferson Smith learns of a conspiracy to rob millions of dollars in taxpayers' money. The plan is to build a giant federal dam on land that has secretly been bought by political insiders. Huge amounts of money are to be pocketed in this boondoggle that is being logrolled through the Congress by Smith's boyhood hero, the state's senior senator. Clued into what's going on, Jefferson Smith commits himself to a do-or-die fight.

Jimmy Stewart plays the junior senator, Jefferson Smith. Claude Rains plays the senior senator, Joseph Paine. A knight in shining armor to the voter, Paine in fact does what he's told by the state's political boss.

What staggered the viewers of *Mr. Smith Goes to Washington* is the conduct of Mr. Smith's Senate colleagues. As seen here, his fellow members of the "world's greatest deliberative body" are as morally comatose as cattle. The members of the press gallery are just as bad. If the senators would rather close their eyes to corruption rather than allow some outsider to disturb the political peace, the reporters' only interest in Jeff Smith is what an ass they can make out of the new kid in the next edition.

The climax is thrilling: Jeff Smith takes the Senate floor all alone to wage a one-man filibuster against the effort by Senator Paine and the party leadership to railroad him. Anyone who's seen it remembers the drained, hanging-on-by-a-hair look he wears on his face while struggling to keep up the fight.

The Washington establishment hated *Mr. Smith,* just as director Frank Capra suspected it might. When the National Press Club offered to sponsor the premiere, he invited its officers to see the picture first.

Given what came next, it's unfortunate that they didn't take up the offer. It might have spared both Washington and Capra a teeth-gnashing night at the movies.

On October 16, 1939, Constitution Hall was packed to the last seat with men and women in formal dress. The outside streets were jammed with limousines. A Marine Band played as Supreme Court justices, Cabinet members, and senators— four thousand people in all—awaited to see a major motion picture they fully expected to reflect their own smug view of public service, i.e., business as usual.

Then, aghast at what they had seen on the screen before them, a full third of the crowd walked out.

The offended Washington big shots had a powerful ally— U.S. Ambassador to the Court of St. James Joseph P. Kennedy. The father of a future president, Kennedy was best known then for backing British Prime Minister Neville Chamberlain's policy of appeasement toward Hitler. The Nazi invasion of Poland that September had made that policy both obsolete and discredited. Unfazed by his historic blindness, Kennedy wired the head of Columbia pictures, Harry Cohn, demanding that he withdraw *Mr. Smith Goes to Washington* from distribution:

> Embassy of the United States
> London, November 17, 1939

> Dear Mr. Cohn:

> I am afraid that we are looking at [*Mr. Smith*] through different eyes. I haven't the slightest doubt that the picture will be successful in America and I have no doubt that financially, it will be successful here and will give great pleasure to people who see it. It is my belief, however, that . . . it will give an idea of our political life that will do us harm. . . .
> . . . I have a high regard for Mr. Capra . . . but his fine work makes the indictment of our government all the more damning to foreign audiences. . . . I feel that to show this film in foreign countries will do inestimable harm to American prestige all over the world. I regret exceedingly that I find it necessary to say these things. . . . The fact remains, however, that pictures from the United States are the greatest influence on foreign public opinion

of the American mode of life. The times are precarious, the future is dark at best. We must be more careful.

Sincerely yours,
Joseph P. Kennedy

The good news is that moviegoers, starting with the critics, loved *Mr. Smith* as much as the Washington crowd had hated it.

"The bewildered young Senator Smith symbolizes those figures who arise occasionally to challenge the dragons," said *The Kansas City Journal*. "Those they would dethrone brand them as radicals and eccentrics and seek to discredit their motives." *Variety* called it "the most vital and stirring drama of contemporary American life yet told on film." Hedda Hopper called it as great as the Gettysburg Address.

"The high privilege of being an American citizen finds its best and most effective expression in *Mr. Smith Goes to Washington*," said the *Cincinnati Post*. The *Los Angeles Times* outdid them all: "It says all the things about America that have been crying out to be said again—and says them beautifully."

The reason for the movie's popularity—then and today—is that it strikes something in the American heart. Just as we take pride in our *self-made* roots and being a place where someone can become who or what they want, we have an equally grand notion of ourselves as *constant rebels*. Who wouldn't want to be that person with the guts to stand alone against the corruption and cynicism of the powers-that-be? Who wouldn't be thrilled to be Jeff Smith standing up for all that's good in democracy against those who would undermine it for the special interests?

What gives Capra's film its hold on the American people is the truth it screams. Corruption is able to take hold because of its appeal to human greed and easy ambition—always abundant resources in Washington, D.C. It offers not only enticements but also rationalizations. Political bosses like the one in *Mr. Smith* figure that every ambitious young politician has a price. It's simply a question of figuring out what that price is.

"Anything that's important to the state is mighty important to me," Boss Taylor declares as he tries seducing the young senator. "Now if I felt that you had the welfare of the state at heart like I do, I'd say you were a man to watch. Now what would you like? Business? If you like business, you can pick any job in the state and go right to the top. Or politics? If you like being a senator, there's no reason why you can't come back to that Senate and stay there as long as you want."

Young Jeff Smith gets the kinder, greater case for corruption from the man he most respects. Listen, as his hero Sena-

tor Joe Paine coaches him on the long-ago deal he himself
once had to cut:

> It's a brutal world, Jeff, and you've no place in it. You'll only get
> hurt. Now take my advice. Forget Taylor and what he said. For-
> get you ever heard of the Willet Creek Dam. I know it's tough to
> run head-on into facts but, well as I said, this is a man's world,
> Jeff, and you've got to check your ideals outside the door, like
> you do your rubbers. Thirty years ago, I had your ideals. I was
> you. I had to make the same decision you were asked to make
> today. And I made it. I compromised—yes! So that all those
> years I could sit in that Senate and serve the people in a thou-
> sand honest ways.
>
> You've got to face facts, Jeff. I've served our state well,
> haven't I? We have the lowest unemployment and the highest
> federal grants. But, well, I've had to compromise. I've had to
> play ball. You can't count on people voting. Half the time they
> don't vote anyway. That's how states and empires have been
> built since time began. Don't you understand? Well, Jeff, you
> can take my word for it. That's how things are. Now I've told
> you all this because, well, I've grown very fond of you. About
> like a son, in fact. And I don't want to see you get hurt.

This is vintage political seduction: there's a bank of enticements placed before the newcomer. There's the stick as
well as the carrot. Play the game and you get ahead; go your

own way and you get hurt. Then comes the kicker: your friends are in on the deal; if you blow it you'll hurt them. Besides, the only way to get things done, good things, is to go along with the sleazy stuff.

Remote from the corridors of political power, unlikely to ever walk in his shoes, audiences grasped instantly what Jeff Smith was up against. They recognized the guts it would take for an ordinary man to stand up to an entrenched system, especially on the floor of the United States Senate surrounded by a cynical room of political insiders, watched over by an equally cynical gaggle up in the press gallery.

All Jeff Smith has going for him is the principles he brought with him from the outside world—in other words, from the country itself.

"You think I'm licked. You all think I'm licked," the exhausted young idealist says as Senator Paine confronts him with cartloads of phony, politically generated letters denouncing him. "Well, I'm not licked, and I'm gonna stay right here and fight this lost cause even if this room gets filled with lies, and the Taylors and all their armies come marching into this place. Somebody'll listen to me."

Those words speak with the enduring voice and soul of America standing up for what it believes in the face of those who would corrupt it. It is the voice, not just of Jefferson Smith but also of young Tom Jefferson and the other passionate men who created this country.

The notion of the *constant rebel,* like that of being *self-made,* was born with the country itself. In January 1776, a young English immigrant, Thomas Paine, wrote a pamphlet titled *Common Sense.* It sold 500,000 copies in a country that had barely two million people.

It made a basic argument: America was a revolutionary-minded country, and its independence was inevitable. It was time to stop the endless effort to accommodate the British and do what had to be done, which was to declare America a separate country.

Six months later, the Continental Congress did just that.

"Government even in its best state is but a necessary evil . . . in its worst state an intolerable one," Paine famously proclaimed in *Common Sense.* And the revolutionary spirit of the country did not die after the Revolution had ended. Tom Paine repeated his sentiments in 1791 with *The Rights of Man.* "Man did not enter into society to become worse than he was before, not to have fewer rights than he had before but to have those rights better secured."

That same year, Thomas Jefferson won approval of the Bill of Rights. These rights included, but were specifically *not* limited to—freedom of religion, speech, press, and assembly; the right to bear arms; the right *not* to have troops quartered in your house; the right *not* to be searched without a warrant; the right *not* to have to testify against yourself; the right to a speedy trial and to be tried by a jury; the right *not* to be cruelly or unusually punished.

There also were included rightful prohibitions on what government could do to the individual citizen. They were constitutional guarantees, not to governmental benefits but to *freedom* from governmental power. They were attempts to stymie the emergence of a new political elite that might seize the privileged positions of power so recently held by the British.

The Bill of Rights was the enduring testament to the fact that, in this newly created nation, government power would be suspected and resisted. That goes for any force that would try to subdue the rights and freedoms of the individual American.

Here the bottom line is rock solid: we favor the individual person against the government.

For better or worse, this is the vintage American view of government. It may be necessary to have a government, but we don't trust it.

We don't want to trust it. We want those in power to worry about *us*.

In a letter he wrote to James Madison in 1787, Thomas Jefferson said, "Unsuccessful rebellions, indeed, generally establish the encroachments on the rights of the people which have produced them. An observation of this truth should render honest republican governors so mild in their punishment of rebellions as not to discourage them too much. It is a medicine necessary for the sound health of the government."

Andrew Jackson

Though he was the seventh president, Andrew Jackson was the first to take up the cause of the little man against the interests of entrenched political and economic power. The majority of Americans of that era saw Jackson, elected president in 1828, as their champion. He was a rough man of the frontier, armed with the grit to fight both Indians and the Eastern banks with equal gusto. To those living in Tennessee, in what was then considered the American West, he was a hero.

Born in 1767, he started his public life as a messenger in the Revolutionary War. After studying law, he moved to Nashville, then still part of North Carolina. He built a successful law practice, became a land speculator, and, at twenty-nine, became the first congressman from the new state of Tennessee.

After later service as a U.S. senator, he was named commander of the state militia. He won the nickname "Old Hickory" during the War of 1812 for ensuring that his entire army of 2,500 men returned home safely from an aborted 1813 mission to New Orleans—thereby disobeying an order to disband the unit in Mississippi.

Jackson added to his reputation in 1815 by returning to New Orleans and this time successfully engaging the British forces. In this, the last action of the War of 1812, he lured the British into attacking his position. They did so at the cost of 2,000 casualties. The American losses were six dead, ten wounded.

Reelected as a U.S. senator from Tennessee in 1823, Jackson ran unsuccessfully for president in 1824. He ran again four years later, this time successfully defeating John Quincy Adams. Once in office, Jackson's biggest target would be the Second Bank of the United States, which he viewed as elitist and undemocratic. After vetoing the Bank Bill in 1832, he ordered his Secretary of the Treasury to withdraw all government money from the institution. When the Cabinet member refused, Jackson fired him.

"The Bank War," writes the historian Arthur Schlesinger, "triumphantly established Jackson in the confidence of the people. Their faith in him had survived ordeals and won vindication: thereafter, when faced by a choice between Jackson and a cherished policy, the voters would choose Jackson."

Jackson was a true democratic hero. As a man of the people, elected to challenge the corrupt marriage of money and politics, he set the standard. "Jackson was widely acclaimed as the symbol of what the new American thought himself to be—a self-made man, son of the frontier, endowed with virtue and God-given strength because of his closeness to nature, and possessed of indomitable will and moral courage," according to Joseph J. Tregle, Jr., a Jackson scholar at Louisiana State University.

Populism

Toward the end of the nineteenth century, the frontier resentment toward the East that had driven Jackson's career gave rise to the American populist movement. The platform of the People's Party called for a progressive income tax and the direct election of U.S. senators—both of which became law within a generation—restrictions on land speculation, and government ownership of railroads and telegraph companies.

The Populists elected a number of candidates to Congress in 1894. Two years later, the Democratic nominee for president, William Jennings Bryan, had taken for his own many of the Populist causes. Bryan's "Cross of Gold" speech, delivered at the Democratic National Convention, endures as an eloquent example of American populist principles. Invoking Old Hickory himself, Bryan berated the wealthy elite and lionized laborers and farmers. "What we need is an Andrew Jackson to stand, as Jackson stood, against the encroachments of organized wealth."

"Upon which side will the Democratic party fight?" Bryan challenged the convention delegates:

Upon the side of "the idle holders of idle capital" or upon the side of "the struggling masses?" You come to us and tell us that the great cities are in favor of the gold standard; we reply that the great cities rest upon our broad and fertile prairies. Burn down your cities and leave our farms, and your cities will spring up again as if by magic; but destroy our farms and the grass will grow in the streets of every city in the country. Our ancestors, when but three millions in number had the courage to declare their political independence of every other nation; shall we, their descendants, when we have grown to seventy millions, declare that we are less independent than our forefathers?

If they dare to come out in the open field and defend the gold standard as a good thing, we will fight them to the uttermost. Having behind us the producing masses of this nation and the world, supported by the commercial interests, the laboring interests and the toilers everywhere, we will answer their demand for a gold standard by saying to them: You shall not press down upon the brow of labor this crown of thorns, you shall not crucify mankind upon a cross of gold.

While never gaining majority support, the Populist agenda met the Jeffersonian prescription of "a little rebellion now and then." Its criticism of the pro-business Republican establishment in the late nineteenth century would become the "medicine" of reform in the early twentieth.

In 1928, Huey Long was elected governor of Louisiana. He became a U.S. senator in 1930. He was a hero to the "little man," a critic of banks and big corporate interests. He called himself "The Kingfish" after a character on the popular "Amos and Andy" radio show. "I'm a small fish here in Washington," he said, "but I'm the Kingfish to the folks down in Louisiana."

The Kingfish pushed a national economic program called "Share the Wealth." It was remarkably simple: every family would be guaranteed $5,000; everyone over age sixty would get an old-age pension; every fortune would be limited to $50 million, inheritances to $5 million, and annual incomes to $1 million.

In order to promote his program, Long relied on grass-roots "Share the Wealth" clubs. The organizations sported the slogan, "Every Man a King, But No One Wears a Crown," a phrase Long borrowed from one of William Jennings Bryan's speeches. A political showman, Long angered his Senate colleagues with his frequent use of the filibuster. But the Senate floor gave Long a platform to push his "Share the Wealth" scheme and to rail against the rich.

Long was famous for his down-home brand of oratory. "How many men ever went to a barbecue and would let one man take off the table what's intended for 9/10ths of the people to eat?" he asked. "The only way to be able to feed the balance of the people is to make that man come back and bring back some of that grub that he ain't got no business with!"

Dismissing Long as a demagogue is too easy. He won the hick vote by pretending to be one of them. He knew how to tap a legitimate vein of deep American resentment. We suspect political and economic power even in good times. When the jobless rate starts to climb, as it did so frighteningly in the thirties, that suspicion, now turned to rage, shows up at the ballot box.

But for most Americans the goal is not to take from the rich and give to the poor. It's to stop the elite from cheating the average citizen of what is rightly his. Former U.S. Labor Secretary Robert Reich calls this our fear of "rot at the top." It is "about the malevolence of powerful elites, be they wealthy aristocrats, rapacious business leaders, or imperious government officials."

Such fist-shaking at "Washington" and "Wall Street" is as American as dumping that tea in Boston Harbor.

"The struggle is only occasionally and incidentally a matter of money or class. There are no workers pitted against capitalists at the heart of this American story," Reich writes. "It is, rather, a tale of corruption, decadence, and irresponsibility among the powerful, of conspiracy against the broader public." As the headlines of 2002 prove, such corruption is still alive in the boardrooms of our largest corporations. Insider trading and dishonest accounting fatten the wallets of CEOs and hurt the little guy, the honest investor.

Resentment toward the powerful runs back, as we have seen, to the days of the Revolution. Abuse of power by the English monarchy prompted our Founding Fathers to adopt a government of checks and balances, grounded in the Enlightenment principle of government through consent. American history has also been characterized by efforts to limit big business, through antitrust laws and labor unions, and to decentralize government, through civil service and electoral reforms.

Despite the anti-"Washington" rhetoric that seems these days to fire every successful presidential campaign, Americans are not blindly against government. Not by any means. We like Social Security because we contribute to it as individuals—we earn our right to those checks after retirement. It's a program custom-made for the American temperament: it doesn't come from the government, it comes from our work and our lifetime of paychecks. It's not welfare because it only goes to people who work and contribute to it.

Government is also good when it comes to our aid in times of crisis. It is not good when it interferes in our daily, often ornery, joy of being Americans.

In a nearly religious way, Americans subscribe to the belief expressed by England's Lord Acton: "Power tends to corrupt; absolute power corrupts absolutely."

We are rebels *by nature*. That word "freedom" is not just in our founding documents; it's in our souls.

We are the most freedom-loving people in the world. We'd rather have guns than live under a government powerful enough to collect them all. We regularly say no to a national health system fearing it means a regime of long lines for strange doctors. Even people with grave concerns about abortion would rather see women individually decide the matter than live under a government repressive enough to deny them the freedom to decide.

Norman Rockwell wonderfully captured this American notion with his 1943 illustration "Freedom of Speech." In it a working man stands all alone at a town meeting where it is clear his words are being taken with respect. This is America at its finest: a guy with a case to make dares to stand up and take the floor.

John McCain

Today, many see U.S. Senator John McCain of Arizona as the personification of the rebel American willing to take on the system. He's a fighter who earned his standing as a prisoner of war in North Vietnam. Although he was repeatedly beaten, abused, and tortured, McCain refused the enemy's offer to be released early.

As he would later write, "I knew that every prisoner the

Vietnamese tried to break, those who had arrived before me and those who would come after me, would be taunted with the story of how an admiral's son had gone home early, a lucky beneficiary of America's class-conscious society. I knew that my release would add to the suffering of men who were already straining to keep faith with their country."

McCain knew the power of such propaganda. He has described how his own faith in his country kept him alive during those horrible five and a half years in the notorious Hanoi Hilton: "It was hard to take our interrogators' ridicule of our conviction that our loyalty to America was returned, measure for measure, by our distant compatriots. But we clung to our belief, each one encouraging the other, not with overexuberant hopes that our day of liberation was close at hand, but with a steady resolve that our honor was the extension of a great nation's honor, and that both prisoner and country would do what honor asked of us."

A student of Machiavelli would recognize why their patriotism and devotion grew steadily. I say this because the greatest bit of wisdom in *The Prince* is that loyalty to a ruler grows in direct proportion to the sacrifices made on his behalf. It's certainly plausible that McCain's five-plus years in a North Vietnamese prison made him more patriotic than before he was shot down.

"In prison, I fell in love with my country," he wrote. "I had loved her before then, but . . . it wasn't until I had lost America for a time that I realized how much I loved her."

There, in a lonely cell somewhere in the middle of a foreign jungle halfway around the world, McCain clung to the part of America that his captors could never take from him. "I still shared the ideals of America. And since those ideals were all that I possessed of my country, they became all the more important to me."

McCain once said that each POW would spend his time using his mind on different projects. Math guys would work on models and proofs. A third-generation Navy man, McCain focused on the countries of the world and where they went wrong. And when he came home, he set out to fix the country for which he had suffered and which he had served so well.

One of the things he has spent his lawmaking career trying to fix is the way we finance political campaigns. The problem begins when politicians start mortgaging themselves to contributors. It is hard to argue with McCain's conviction that much of what is wrong in national policy-making results from the distortion of the piper calling the tune.

McCain's election to the U.S. Congress and the U.S. Senate, his gutsy campaign for the presidency in 2000, and his successful fight for campaign reform in 2002 are right out of *Mr. Smith Goes to Washington.* He is the outsider standing up to the inside, the reformer fighting the system.

But most important, he is the idealist confronting the cynics.

In 2002, John McCain launched a new rebellion against what he branded "crony capitalism." He called for far tougher measures than those proposed by either President George W. Bush or many Democrats. "Trust was sacrificed in too many corporate boardrooms on the altar of quick and illusory profits."

John McCain knows that the American people, by nature rebellious, recoil most at being made to feel powerless. That, of course, was the spirit of *Mr. Smith Goes to Washington.*

Joe Kennedy worried that it would make people in war-torn Europe think *less* of American democracy. He could not have been more wrong.

Those last words of Jefferson Smith on the Senate floor still hold power:

> Just get up off the ground. That's all I ask. Get up there with that lady, that's up on top of this Capitol Dome. That lady that stands for Liberty. Take a look at this country through her eyes if you really want to see somethin'. And you won't just see scenery. You'll see the whole parade of what man's carved out for himself after centuries of fighting. And fighting for something better than just jungle law. Fighting so he can stand on his own two feet free and decent, like he was created no matter what his race, color, or creed. That's what you'd see. There's no place out there for graft or greed or lies! Or compromise with human liberties! Great principles don't get lost once they come to light. They're right here. You just have to see them again. . . .

In November of 1942, the occupying Nazis issued a ban preventing theaters throughout France from showing any American or British films. French theaters chose Frank Capra's *Mr. Smith* as the last English-language film to be shown before the ban went into effect. According to the Army News Service, one theater played *Mr. Smith Goes to Washington* every day for a month.

This is from the November 4 edition of the *Hollywood Reporter:*

> Storms of spontaneous applause broke out at the sequence when, under the Abraham Lincoln monument in the capital, the word "Liberty" appeared on the screen and the Stars and Stripes began fluttering over the head of the great Emancipator in the cause of liberty. Similarly cheers and acclamation punctuated the famous speech of the young senator on man's rights and dignity.

"It was . . . as though the joys, suffering, love and hatred, the hopes and wishes of an entire people who value freedom above everything, found expression for the last time."

CHAPTER 3

The Reluctant Warrior

It occurred to me that the Rattle-Snake is found in no
other quarter of the world besides America.

BENJAMIN FRANKLIN, 1775

If you're an American, your favorite movie is probably
Casablanca. At least, that's what the surveys show. When
you think of it, it's hard to beat Humphrey Bogart as a world-
weary nightclub owner in an exotic locale carrying a torch for
the translucently beautiful Ingrid Bergman.

But there's something else that locks this movie in our
dreams. It's about us. It's about an American guy torn by his
passion for a lost love and the need to fight a triumphant
Nazism that threatens everything he holds dear. The
Wehrmacht has overrun Europe. World War II is raging, the
United States is still neutral, and here's this Yank running a
bar in a North African city that's become a haven for
refugees. He, too, is a refugee from the war and from the
memory of a girl he loved and lost in Paris.

The movie script gives his name as Rick Blaine. But it's the rogue persona of Humphrey Bogart that jumps off the screen. That's what plays in our memory. In a very tough situation, he's standing in for us at our best. He will fight when he has to and not a moment sooner. Until then, he sits out the war in Vichy-controlled Morocco.

"I stick my neck out for nobody," he says when the collaborationist local police chief arrests one of the regulars at Rick's Café, mainly in order to impress a newly arrived SS officer. Rick refuses to show concern even when this odious Major Strasser boasts of soon catching the great resistance leader Victor Lazslo.

"Excuse me, gentleman, your business is politics," he says, getting up to leave. "Mine is running a saloon."

It's only when there's talk of attacking America that our hero begins to suggest the stuff he's made of.

MAJOR STRASSER: Can you imagine us in London?

RICK: When you get there, ask me.

MAJOR STRASSER: How about New York?

RICK: Well there are certain sections of New York, Major, that I wouldn't advise you to try to invade.

Now our guy is showing his teeth. His ideals, his love, and his country all on the line, Rick will commit himself to the war against an evil he now sees in its face.

"I'm no good at being noble," he bids farewell to his beloved Ilsa, who he's learned is the wife of Victor Lazslo, "but it doesn't take much to see that the problems of three little people don't amount to a hill of beans in this crazy world."

There's a fine reason why *Casablanca* is the most cherished American movie of all time. It *gets* to us Americans, stays with us, for the basic reason that it strikes at something deep in us. We're proud to live in a country where every neighborhood, especially those "certain sections of New York," would go toe-to-toe with the *SS*. We're proud of an American guy who knows what's worth fighting for and what isn't.

This grand American notion of the *reluctant warrior* is a theme that we've treasured from our beginnings. We are not a country that's ever been impressed by generals in epaulets and high-peaked hats. Our officers don't strut. Our troops don't goosestep. We deride a Fidel Castro who parades about in his rebel fatigues decades after the revolution has lost its zing. But while we reject the dandified haberdashery of war, we will strike back ferociously when attacked, when someone or something we value dearly is threatened.

"Don't Tread on Me"

On September 11, 2001, New York firefighters offered their lives by racing up the steps of the World Trade Center towers as thousands raced down to safety. "This is my job," said one brave fireman as he saw the question in the passing woman's eyes. Meanwhile, in the skies over Pennsylvania a brave passenger yelled "Let's roll!" as he and others rushed the cockpit. Why should we fear even a dangerous world when we have men like these?

There was also the reaction of our new, untested president. "This nation is peaceful, but fierce when stirred to anger," he said to a hushed audience in the National Cathedral that first Friday.

Hours later he stood amid the rubble of the World Trade Center, his arm slung over the shoulder of an older fire-

fighter. "We can't hear you!" someone yelled from the crowd. "I can hear *you*!" he yelled back through a bullhorn. "The rest of the world hears you, and the people who knocked these buildings down will hear all of us soon!" At that moment Bush became president to all Americans. What the Supreme Court could not accomplish in December of 2000, this flash of fighting spirit did.

Our fierce reaction to the events of September 11 has been compared to the U.S. response to the Japanese attack on Pearl Harbor in December 1941. Both times the country was caught off guard. Both times we understood what our history expected of us.

Even back before the stars and stripes, we had a battle flag that rallied us and warned our enemies. On it was a coiled rattlesnake atop a bright yellow background, with the words "Don't Tread on Me" emblazoned underneath. Nicknamed the "Gadsden Flag" for the South Carolina patriot Christopher Gadsden, it was quickly adopted as the standard of the then-fledgling Continental Navy. It was first flown in December 1775, not yet one full year into the Revolution.

Although the Gadsden Flag remains the most famous "Don't Tread on Me" image, it wasn't the rattlesnake's only appearance during the Revolution. Marines in the Continental army were inspired to paint the same serpent on the sides of their drums as they marched into battle.

Benjamin Franklin was struck by the insignia's message:

I observed on one of the drums belonging to the marines now
raising up there was painted a Rattle-Snake, with the modest
motto under it, "Don't Tread on Me." It occurred to me that the
Rattle-Snake is found in no other quarter of the world besides
America. She has no eyelids. She may therefore be esteemed an
emblem of vigilance. She never begins an attack, nor, when once
engaged, ever surrenders: She is therefore an emblem of magna-
nimity and true courage. The weapons with which nature has
furnished her she conceals in the roof of her mouth so that, to
those who are unacquainted with her, she appears to be a most
defenseless animal. And even when those weapons are shown
and extended for her defense, they appear weak and con-
temptible; but their wounds, however small, are decisive and
fatal. Conscious of this, she never wounds 'till she has generously given notice, even to her enemy, and cautioned him
against the danger of treading on her.

Was I wrong, Sir, in thinking this a strong picture of the tem-
per and conduct of America?

"The Rattle-Snake is solitary, and associates with her kind
only when it is necessary for their preservation," Franklin
adds. This menacing icon of America's independent nature
symbolizes the instinct to ally with others when faced with a
common danger.

George Washington

During the American Revolution, the artist Benjamin West was asked by King George III what he thought George Washington, the leader of the American revolutionaries, would do after the war. When West answered that Washington would return to his Virginia farm, the king replied, "If he does that, he will be the greatest man in the world."

As much as the "Don't Tread on Me" flag and its accompanying rattlesnake, as much as Rick Blaine in *Casablanca,* Washington personifies the reluctant warrior. His victories at Trenton and Princeton not only kept the Continental army in the field, they kept his young country in the war. That brilliant campaign of retreat along the Delaware, his courage in the winter at Valley Forge, and his final triumph at Yorktown hold an illustrious place in military history.

But it was Washington's quiet retirement to his plantation on the Potomac that most made him a noble model for the new republic. Once he had led his troops to victory against the British, he returned with dispatch to his beloved Mount Vernon. Called back in 1789 to become his country's first president, he again set an example of disinterested service by limiting his tenure to two terms.

The *manner* of his second retirement was also standard-setting. In the autumn of 1796, he submitted an article to a Philadelphia daily newspaper, then spent the following weekend correcting the proofs. In this, his farewell address to "the People of the United States; Friends and Fellow Citizens," Washington made three points.

First, he said he would not seek reelection to a third term. Second, he thanked the country for the honors it conferred on him and the confidence it had shown in him. Third, he issued a warning that said, in effect: Don't allow America to be sucked into becoming some other country's easy ally or automatic enemy:

> The Nation which indulges toward another an habitual hatred or an habitual fondness, is in some degree a slave. It is a slave to its animosity or to its affection, with of which is sufficient to lead it astray from its duty and its interest. Therefore, it must be unwise in us to implicate ourselves by artificial ties in the ordinary vicissitudes of her politics, or the ordinary combinations and collisions of her friendships or enmities.

Washington believed that the strength of a country's readiness to fight necessary wars is fortified by its readiness to return to peaceful endeavors once the last necessary shot has been fired. It was a philosophy he had eloquently articulated twenty years earlier, during the height of the Revolution itself. "I shall constantly bear in mind that as the sword was the last resort for the preservation of our liberties, so it ought to be the first to be laid aside when those liberties are firmly established," he had written from New Jersey in 1777.

Even as Washington made a dramatic point of withdrawing swiftly to Mount Vernon, he advised his country to draw back in the same way from "permanent alliances" that could lead us into other countries' wars: " 'Tis our true policy to steer clear of permanent alliances with any portion of the foreign world." He wanted America to play the field and avoid getting hooked up with one or the other European power, either England or France.

"In a word, I want an *American* character that the powers of Europe may be convinced we act for ourselves and not for others," he said simply.

"No one better taught than Washington that the sword is readiest for its proper use when most swiftly relinquished after the crisis is over," noted biographer Garry Wills. "He never glorified the sword. His own scheme of ornamentation at Mount Vernon was peaceful and rustic—he directed that a dove of peace, with its olive in its mouth, be used as weather vane."

Washington despised the pomp and opulence of the British royal court, and determined from the beginning to set a new model. A heroic general who could have made himself dictator for life, he calmly abdicated the spoils and laurels of victory for the freedom and dignity of private citizenship.

"When we assumed the Soldier, we did not lay aside the

Citizen," he wrote to the New York legislature in 1775, "and we shall most sincerely rejoice with you in that happy hour when the establishment of American Liberty, upon the most firm and solid foundations, shall enable us to return to our Private Stations in the bosom of a free, peaceful and happy Country."

Translation: Excuse me, gentlemen, your business is politics. Mine is running a plantation.

Thomas Jefferson

On taking the presidential oath in March 1801, Thomas Jefferson reaffirmed the ideal set by George Washington. Like the first president, he wanted to keep the young republic clear of the perennially raging war between Britain and France. "Peace, commerce and honest friendship with all nations; entangling alliances with none," Jefferson promised in his first inaugural.

At the time a small country, America would inevitably be the unlucky pawn if dragged into a war between the two early nineteenth-century superpowers. Though Jefferson favored democratic France against royalist Britain, he realized that the new republic's survival hinged on staying neutral.

The brilliant Jefferson's warning about "entangling alliances" would hold sway for a century. This policy of staying clear of European conflicts, of sticking to our business and own wars, continued right up until World War I.

The United States had done everything it could to stay neutral. Our slow entry into the great European conflict, which President Woodrow Wilson sold as a war to make the world "safe for democracy," was followed by an eager desire to return home swiftly at war's end.

"America's present need is not heroics, but healing; not nostrums, but normalcy," Warren Harding declared during his successful presidential bid of 1920. No entangling alliances for him either.

World War II

"If it's December 1941 in Casablanca," Bogie's character asks his piano player Sam, "what time is it in New York? I bet they're asleep in New York. I'll bet they're asleep all over America."

But not for long. Thanks to the sneak Japanese attack on our Hawaiian naval base at Pearl Harbor, America was about to "get involved" in World War II. Like the coiled rattlesnake of the American Revolution we were about to strike back with vengeance.

In a wild coincidence, *Casablanca* was released in the same month, November 1942, that the real city of Casablanca was being liberated by American troops. The following February, President Franklin D. Roosevelt and British Prime Minister Winston Churchill met there to map out plans for the invasion of France.

Roosevelt and Churchill would also forge an alliance with the "Free French" forces of General Charles de Gaulle. Until then, President Roosevelt had maintained relations with the collaborationist French regime in hopes that its troops in North Africa would join with the Allies. This pretense died that same November 1942 when Vichy forces in North Africa offered resistance to the Allied invasion.

Casablanca ends with the start of a "beautiful friendship" between the American Rick Blaine and the French police chief played by Claude Rains (who also played Senator Paine in *Mr. Smith Goes to Washington*). Both of them have now joined the fight. It's hard not be struck by the real-life parallel. As a result of the Casablanca Conference, the United States and France renewed an alliance that began in the American Revolution and lives to this day.

Writing about *Casablanca* and the character of Rick Blaine in *America in the Movies,* the critic Michael Wood notes the connection between Rick's desire to steer clear of World War II with the warnings of both Washington and Jefferson: "I want to suggest that there is in America a *dream of freedom* which appears in many places and many forms, which lies somewhere at the back of several varieties of isolationism and behind whatever we mean by individualism, which converts selfishness from something of a vice into something of a virtue, and which confers a peculiar, gleaming prestige on loneliness. It is a dream of freedom from others; it is a fear, to use a sanctioned and favorite word, of entanglement. It is what we mean when we say, in our familiar phrase, that we don't want to get *involved*."

Casablanca would reclaim its hold on Americans, especially young Americans, during the 1960s. Faced with the war in Vietnam and the draft, college students identified with Bogart's Rick Blaine, the guy who refused to fight unless something truly important was at stake. Many college students didn't think Vietnam met that test. Starting at Harvard Square's Brattle Theatre, a cult was born.

Popular culture-watcher Henry Allen has sought to explain it. "It might not have acquired its cult status if it hadn't been for the assassination of Kennedy, with his witty tough-guy appeal, and the Vietnam War, which made us hunger for a time when there were things worth dying for."

The Powell Doctrine

The catastrophe of Vietnam led to the desire to avoid future American military interventions that lacked strong popular support, a winnable mission and an "exit strategy."

But before new rules of American engagement could be codified, the United States would suffer one more military humiliation.

In 1983, a car bomber slaughtered 241 Marines stationed in Beirut. Most of the victims died in their sleep. Aghast at the carnage, Americans asked how a contingent of troops sent in as "peacemakers" had become targets and belligerents.

One explanation for the disaster was that Ronald Reagan, then the Commander in Chief, had accepted bad advice. He had been sold the idea that American troops could be seen as neutral in a conflict that had our ally Israel on one side and Lebanese militants on the other. Sent in as a "peacekeeping" force, our Marines were given the in-your-face job of policing Beirut International Airport, which made them irresistible targets. Fired on, they were forced to fire back, which had the effect of making them despised throughout the Arab world.

What would become known as the "Powell Doctrine" arose in response to the disaster in Beirut. With memories of the Vietnam horror still painful, Secretary of Defense Caspar Weinberger and his chief military assistant General Colin Powell drafted new criteria for overseas military involvement. War, they agreed, should be a *last resort*. It should be undertaken only in the presence of *precise political and military goals* with clear *popular support* from the American public and the Congress. There must be a clear *exit strategy*, and an unhesitating will to deploy *overwhelming force*.

The Powell Doctrine reconciled America's new status as the lone superpower with its reluctant-warrior past.

"War should be the politics of last resort," Powell wrote in his autobiography. "And when we go to war, we should have a purpose that our people understand and support; we should mobilize the country's resources to fulfill that mission and then go in to win. In Vietnam, we had entered into a half-hearted half-war, with much of the nation opposed or indifferent, while a small fraction carried the burden."

Powell condemned the ambiguous mission objectives that led to the 1983 Lebanon fiasco:

When the political objective is important, clearly defined and understood, when the risks are acceptable, and when the use of force can be effectively combined with diplomatic and economic policies, then clear and unambiguous objectives must be given to armed forces. These objectives must be firmly linked with the political objectives. We must not, for example, send military forces into a crisis with an unclear mission they cannot accomplish—such as we did when we sent the U.S. Marines into Lebanon in 1983. We inserted those proud warriors into the middle of a five-faction civil war complete with terrorists, hostage-takers and a dozen spies in every camp, and said, "Gentlemen, be a buffer." . . . When we use force we should not be equivocal; we should win and win decisively.

The great danger lies in sending American troops for a narrowly defined mission, only to see their role expand once in the field. The term is "mission creep." It is among the hazards of foreign intervention the Powell Doctrine was meant to prevent.

A career soldier, Colin Powell was born in Harlem, raised in the South Bronx, and attended the City College of New York, where he enlisted in the ROTC. Twice sent to Vietnam, he was wounded in his first tour, then received the Soldier's Medal for bravery in his second for pulling men from a burning helicopter.

Powell's big break came with his selection to be a White House Fellow during the Nixon administration. This brought him to the Office of Management and Budget and to the attention of a powerful Republican pair: budget director Cap Weinberger and his deputy Frank Carlucci. After serving as Weinberger's aide through the early '80s and later commanding troops in Europe. Powell became Carlucci's deputy and eventually his replacement as director of the National Security Council.

In 1989, General Powell's new Commander-in-Chief, George H.W. Bush, promoted him to the chairmanship of the

Joint Chiefs of Staff. In his first year as chairman, Powell won credit for carrying out the raid on Panama that captured the drug-dealing strongman Manuel Noriega. In the years 1990–91, Powell oversaw the deft planning and lightning execution of the Persian Gulf War to liberate Kuwait from Saddam Hussein's Iraq.

In October 1993, however, U.S. forces found themselves in yet another quagmire overseas. This time the place was Mogadishu, Somalia. Faced with heart-wrenching televised images of starving Africans, President George Bush had sent a contingent of U.S. forces to deliver food to that Horn of Africa nation. But, as the months passed, and the Clinton administration came into office, we Americans took upon ourselves the fateful task of separating the good guys from the bad over there in that remote corner of a continent where we were far from home.

One of the villains was the warlord Farah Aidid, whose capture soon was a U.S. priority. A humanitarian mission had turned into something far different. In a crazed firefight in downtown Mogadishu, under fire from thousands of armed Somalis, eighteen Americans were killed and eighty-four others were wounded. One American's body was dragged through the streets to the delight of the crowd, the voyeuristic gaze of the international media, and the blood-curdling outrage of millions of Americans.

Thomas Jefferson could have predicted it. The readiness of the United States to entangle itself in a civil war on the other side of the globe had cost us lives and dignity. Following the massacre in Mogadishu, the "Powell Doctrine" struck the American people—and especially our military—with a new force.

The Reluctant Warrior Today

In the months after terrorists attacked the World Trade Center and the Pentagon, America was called to arms. The Congress immediately gave President George W. Bush the authority "to use all necessary and appropriate force against those nations, organizations, or persons he determines planned, authorized, committed, or aided the terrorist attacks . . . or harbored such organizations or persons."

Speaking to Congress, Bush was, indeed, the consummate rattlesnake. "The nation is peaceful but *fierce* when stirred to anger."

Sadly, a campaign focused on eradicating the terrorist network behind September 11 soon began to show undeniable signs of mission creep. From a war to destroy Al Qaeda, our target expanded to any international terrorist group.

"We will direct every resource at our command," Bush said, "every means of diplomacy, every tool of intelligence, every instrument of law enforcement, every financial influence, and every necessary weapon of war—to the disruption and to the defeat of the global terror network."

In his 2002 State of the Union speech, Bush pushed the envelope further. He branded three countries—Iran, Iraq, and North Korea—the "axis of evil." He went on, "By seeking weapons of mass destruction, these regimes pose a grave and growing danger. They could provide these arms to terrorists, giving them the means to match their hatred. They could attack our allies or attempt to blackmail the United States."

Just a few weeks later, a high-ranking State Department official appended the names of three other countries—Libya, Syria and Cuba—to the "axis." Sudan and Somalia were soon added to the list of Bush administration targets. From *the* terrorists of September 11, the list had grown, first, to *all* terrorists, then to *all* countries who aid terrorists, then to *all* those thought to be acquiring biological, chemical, or nuclear weapons who might give them to the terrorists.

The list would grow further still. In June 2002, the president proposed to the West Point graduating class that military force might be employed against any country on any continent ruled by "tyrants," that denies "human liberty," that is not "free and open."

Deterrence forgotten, America would now stand ready to take *preemptive action*. This was mission creep with a vengeance.

Myself, I worry that this change in course threatens us with dangerous consequences. Will America still be guided by its role as a reluctant warrior in this new century? Or will the reality of America's colossal military power overwhelm the fine instincts of its history?

CHAPTER 4

Action

Shift that fat ass, Harry. But slowly, or you'll swamp
the damned boat.

GENERAL GEORGE WASHINGTON TO COLONEL
HENRY KNOX, DECEMBER 25, 1776

Americans trust brainpower only so far. Our admiration
runs most naturally to the activist, the person who's out there
showing not just what he thinks but what he can do.

Ernest Hemingway

When we think of American novelists, Ernest Hemingway
dominates the landscape. Who else inspires annual contests
to ape his writing style? Every summer American college
students still head to the Left Bank cafés the great man fre-
quented, and even jaded businessmen traveling to Paris
peep into the Hemingway Bar at the Ritz Hotel. People go to
their first bullfight because Hemingway wrote so vividly

about the *corridas*. They head to Africa for safaris because he once did.

Because of him, they often dare to dream of trying their hand at that great American novel.

Why are we so drawn to Hemingway?

Because his genius was to live it, then to write it. He made his readers feel they had done something truly adventurous just by reading his books. This may seem old hat now—but it wasn't back then. There was, in fact, a movie entitled *Wrestling Ernest Hemingway* about a dying old man whose great bragging right was that he had once actually wrestled Papa Hemingway.

Hemingway always had a vision of the life he'd lead. Adventure was the magnet. "I desire to do pioneering or exploring work in the three last great frontiers," he wrote at the tender age of fifteen, "Africa, Southern Central South America or the country around and north of Hudson's Bay."

Not long after, he had his first job as a reporter, covering crime, fires, labor strikes. Using the stylebook of his paper, the *Kansas City Star,* he taught himself to write the short, declarative sentences that he would make his literary trademark.

In World War I, Hemingway volunteered as an ambulance driver. While delivering supplies to the front he was hit by a mortar, taking over twenty fragments of shrapnel in his legs. Then, carrying a more seriously wounded man to the rear, he was sprayed by machine gun bullets. As he lay convalescing in a Red Cross hospital, he was nominated for the Italian medal of honor and was trumpeted in headlines back home as the first American casualty in Italy.

While recuperating—and enjoying himself immensely in the process—Hemingway fell in love with his nurse. Agnes von Kurowsky was twenty-six and the dream girl of every wounded soldier in the ward. Hemingway had just turned nineteen. Though she would ultimately reject his attentions—"I can't get away from the fact that you're just a boy"—the young man from Illinois had gotten what he needed from the experience.

Hemingway returned home, a writer with a story to tell.

Like Teddy Roosevelt, another great American man of action, Ernest Hemingway was his own best biographer. Though only in his teens, he was able to describe what it felt like to be wounded in combat. "Then there was a flash, as when a blast-furnace door is swung open, and a roar that started white and went red and on and on in a rushing wind. I tried to breathe but my breath would not come and I felt myself rush bodily out of myself and out and out and out and all the time bodily in the wind. I went out swiftly, all of myself, and I knew I was dead and that it had all been a mistake to think you just died."

What other writers tried to imagine Hemingway made sure he knew first hand.

Thanks to his war service, Hemingway won a job working in Paris for the *Toronto Star.* He joined the tight-knit community of expatriate writers living on the Left Bank. It turned out to be the right move. "If he hadn't been in Paris when he was," argues biographer Michael Reynolds. "I'm not sure he would have turned out to be the Hemingway we know."

In a short two years, he began to morph into the figure of literary legend.

He saw his first bullfight in 1923—but it was far from his last. His greatest novel, *The Sun Also Rises,* and, years later, his best work of nonfiction, *Death in the Afternoon,* were the result of his immersion in the glamorous but deadly world of the matador.

Hemingway had craved to know fully the people and places he wrote about. It was his competitive edge and he kept it sharp. He never stopped living right up against the characters he wrote about. In *Death in the Afternoon,* Hemingway revealed:

I was trying to write then and I found the greatest difficulty, aside from knowing what you really felt, rather than what you were supposed to feel and had been taught to feel, was to put down what really happened in action; what the actual things were which produced the emotion that you experienced. . . . The only place where you see life and death, i.e., violent death now that the wars were over, was in the bull ring and I wanted very much to go to Spain where I could study it. I was trying to learn to write, commencing with the simplest things, and one of the simplest things of all and the most fundamental is violent death.

His friend Malcolm Cowley observed that, after the publication of the *The Sun Also Rises* in 1926, young Americans "drank like his heroes and heroines, cultivated a hard-boiled melancholy and talked in page after page of Hemingway dialogue." A first generation of disciples had been created.

Next came Africa. In 1933, Hemingway took a ten-week safari to what was then Tanganyika. Sleeping under the immense Africa sky, hunting lion and rhino, he discovered the magic of the Serengeti. Always restless to prove himself in a new and dangerous terrain, Hemingway now had a continent under his belt.

Three years later, when the Spanish Civil War broke out, Hemingway supported the left-wing Loyalists against the rightist forces of General Francisco Franco. With Stalin backing the Loyalist cause and Hitler and Mussolini backing Franco, the war served as a stark prelude to World War II. Traveling with an American volunteer brigade committed to the elected government, Hemingway crafted *For Whom the Bell Tolls*.

Living in Cuba in the 1950s, he wrote the story of an old peasant who struggles with a gargantuan swordfish for four days and nights only to lose him to the sharks. Hemingway called *The Old Man and the Sea* "the best I can write ever for all of my life." It was, he said, "an epilogue to all my writing and what I have learned, or tried to learn, while writing and trying to live. It will kill the school of criticism that claims I can write about nothing except myself and my own experiences." Indeed, the book won the Pulitzer Prize and helped him gain the Nobel Prize for Literature.

No one took keener note of the Hemingway example than Norman Mailer, who would often apply literal muscle to his own prose. Here's what he had to say:

> Let any of you decide for yourselves how silly would be *A Farewell to Arms* or better, *Death in the Afternoon,* if it had been written by a man who was five-four, had acne, wore glasses, spoke in a shrill voice, and was a physical coward. That, of course, is an impossible hypothesis—such a man would never have been able to feel the emotions of the man who wrote that early prose. . . . Without a sense of the big man who wrote the prose, all the later work would be only skeletons of abstraction, the flash gone.

Or listen to *The New York Times:*

> Ernest Hemingway became and remains an American icon and one embodiment of America's promise: the young boy from Oak Park who set out to become the best writer of his time, and did

just that. His ambition, intensity, creative drive, sense of duty, belief in hard work, and faith in the strenuous life carried him to the pinnacle of his profession and provided him with worldwide recognition and considerable wealth before destroying him when he could no longer meet the demands of his public life. It is an old story, older than written words, a story the ancient Greeks would have recognized. Hemingway told us that pursuit was happiness, and that any story followed far enough would end badly. He lived constantly on the edge of the American experience and constantly in the public eye. He wrote books that influenced two or more generations, and was awarded not only with prizes, including the Pulitzer and the Nobel, but with fame such as few writers have known or have had to endure. At the end of the next century, the basic human struggle with universal demons that Hemingway put down with such clarity will still be read, and men may still take heart, knowing that they are not the first nor the last to face their fate.

The simple fact is that Hemingway made it look easy. That's what grabs us: the masculine adventures, the plainness of his style, the boozy exploits, and, of course, the beard. If the truth about Papa was more complicated than that—and the psychobabble never quits—it doesn't matter.

What does matter is his great writer's knack for bringing the action to the reader and with it, the participation in an actual human experience. Here's how he lets us know what it feels to be Jake Barnes, a guy who loves a girl but cannot show it, who night after night must leave her in the company of losers while he heads home alone:

> I went out onto the sidewalk and walked down toward the Boulevard St. Michel, passed the tables of the Rotonde, still crowded, looked across the street at the Dome, its tables running out to the edge of the pavement. Some one waved at me from a table. I did not see who it was and went on. I wanted to get home. The Boulevard Montparnasse was deserted. Lavigne's was closed tight, and they were stacking the tables outside the Closerie des Lilas. . . . My flat was just across the street, a little way down the Boulevard St. Michel.

Barnes is the guy who knows all the parties he hasn't been invited to.

Bush vs. Gore

The American urge to be on the move, forever demanding an audience for our achievements, made Ernest Hemingway an American natural.

Our faith in the value of action began with the frontier. For better or worse, run a cowboy against a dude for president and the cowboy wins. The guy with the sun in his face invariably beats the indoor candidate.

That has never been truer than in the politics of our new American century.

In the 2000 election, Al Gore held powerful advantages. The economy was the strongest in history. The stock market was booming and everybody seemed to be in it. Inflation was so low no one talked about it. Gore, the vice president, enjoyed the best possible credentials to be elected to extend the boom of the previous eight years. While Bill Clinton had embarrassed the presidency and suffered impeachment for his attempted cover-up of an affair with a young White House intern, Gore himself was viewed as a solid, faithful, and loving family man.

So why didn't he eat Bush's lunch? One reason is that Governor George W. Bush, son of the former president, trumped Gore's considerable edge with something Gore couldn't match.

Bush was the cowboy in the race, the guy who wore boots and loved nothing better than kicking back at his ranch in Crawford, Texas.

Gore, despite his roots in Tennessee, came across as the city slicker. Bush had an easy stride and impressed us with who he was. Gore came across to voters as a know-it-all, a guy who had done all his homework but was hesitant to act. Bush was the man on horseback, Gore the guy riding up on the buckboard.

The murkiness of the 2000 election's outcome, including

the U.S. Supreme Court's ruling in Bush's favor on the Florida recount, cannot obscure the fact that Gore blew a race he should have aced.

Actually, George W. Bush did not become the nation's true leader until the Friday after September 11, 2001. It was the sight of him standing on the rubble of the World Trade Center that won him his full legitimacy. Here was an American leader come to lead his people in a cause as righteous as it was necessary.

Hemingway called it "grace under pressure," and there are few things we Americans love more as a nation than watching our president display it.

We tend to entrust the job of commander in chief to someone who's proved his stuff along the way. The battlefield is but one possible arena. We simply like leaders who've undergone genuine rites of passage, whether in log cabins or on PT boats.

George Washington

We saw how George Washington refused to convert his role as Revolutionary commander in chief into a lifetime dictatorship. America would be spared a Napoleon. But there's little doubt that it was his triumphs as a soldier that made him the obvious popular choice for first president.

Hadn't he led us as we defeated the most powerful mili-

tary force on the face of the earth? Thanks to his strategy, sacrifice, and raw guts, this Virginia planter and veteran of the French and Indian War was the British army's worst nightmare.

That final American victory over General Cornwallis at Yorktown could never have been achieved were it not for Washington's incredible feats earlier, especially those legendary victories at Trenton and Princeton. "Lord Cornwallis once observed after Yorktown that the military fame of George Washington would rest not on the Chesapeake but on the Delaware. It was that marvelous bitter, nerve-racking campaign that revealed the fortitude and constancy of the American leader." That's Winston Churchill writing, and it takes one great leader to know another.

In the beginning, Washington made a classic mistake:

he attempted to take the stronger, better-trained, better-disciplined British forces head on. The Battle of Long Island was a disaster. Had he not quickly and shrewdly evacuated the Continental army to Manhattan, that early battle fought in what is today's Brooklyn might easily have been the war's last.

The retreat bought time for the Continental army. But as Churchill was to note in equally dire circumstances two centuries later, wars are not won by evacuations. Falling back through New Jersey, where he found little citizen support, Washington ended up in Pennsylvania desperately needing a victory.

The young country was demanding action. And Washington was ready to give it to them. On Christmas evening 1776, a group of twenty armed Colonials emerged from the woods and attacked a Hessian outpost in Trenton. An hour later, the main force of Americans began crossing the icy, sleet-pelted Delaware River in force, transporting eighteen cannon one at a time on their single flatboat. The officer in charge of logistics was the brilliant Colonel Henry Knox, who had managed to haul the cannon down from the captured Fort Ticonderoga. He was a huge man, standing 6 foot three inches and weighing 280 pounds.

"Shift that fat ass, Harry," Washington teased him as they made the crossing meant to change everything, "but slowly or you'll swamp the damned boat."

With Knox's potent firepower aboard, the attacking forces surrounded and defeated the Hessians. Nine hundred and eighteen were taken prisoner, twenty-one killed. Only one American was killed and only two were wounded.

Washington would follow this victory with another morale builder at Princeton. Angered by the first, humiliating defeat at Trenton, the new Hessian commander warned his troops to take no prisoners. They were to kill any rebel they got their hands on, whether he surrendered or not, or else suffer a reward of fifty lashes for every surviving Continental soldier.

News of the Trenton defeat also brought Cornwallis to the scene. With Washington still at Trenton, the British general saw a rare opportunity to trap the American commander with his back to the Delaware River. But after spotting the enemy campfires below him, the tired British general unwisely chose to spend the night on the high ground and attack in the morning.

"We've got the old fox safe now," he announced. "We'll go over and bag him in the morning. The damned rebels are cornered at last."

Famous last words. Leaving his campfires aglow to confuse the enemy, the American commander in chief led his forces around Cornwallis to attack Princeton, which the British had left unprotected. This second victory humiliated Cornwallis, along with his regular British troops and the Hessians.

Washington was executing a strategy as brilliant as it was necessary. Through daring raids and calculated retreat, he was keeping his army together long enough to outlast the British and win the backing of the French for the climactic battle at Yorktown. He was proving himself not only a skilled fighter but also a shrewd politician.

As the obvious choice for president of the new republic, George Washington also turned out to be the right one.

Andrew Jackson

The Battle of New Orleans clinched it for Andrew Jackson. The climax of that military encounter was a British frontal assault on the American lines. Concentrated cannon and rifle fire from the city's defenders cost the attackers almost two thousand dead and injured. The Americans lost only six with 10 wounded. In the election of 1828, voters wagered that Jackson's military exploits were a harbinger of strong executive leadership. The fact of his historic, activist presidency proved it a good bet.

William Henry Harrison

The electorate's gamble of 1840 was less successful. Anxious to win the White House after twelve years of Democratic rule, the Whigs nominated William Henry Harrison. The candidate's sole credential was his putative military achievement at a place called Tippecanoe Creek in 1811. Surprised by Indians, General Harrison's army forces had suffered significant casualties before driving off their attackers.

Yet it was this excursion—its outcome far from glorious—that gave Harrison victory over Daniel Webster and Henry Clay. For his running mate the Whigs chose former Senator John Tyler of Virginia. (Hence the memorable slogan: "Tippecanoe and Tyler too.") But, apart from that one questionable military exploit in the remote Northwest, Harrison's chief campaign asset was the silence he managed to maintain.

In fact, the Whigs didn't even bother to write a platform. As instructed by the party chiefs, their candidate kept mum on such issues as slavery, the tariff, and the U.S. Bank. His military background and that alliterative catch-phrase were all he had going for him. They turned out to be enough: Harrison and Tyler won by a landslide.

Sadly for Harrison and the country that chose him, on a cold, wet Inaugural Day he developed pneumonia and was dead within the month. His anemic triumph at Tippecanoe had presaged his presidency; *neither* amounted to much.

Ulysses S. Grant

In 1868, the Civil War concluded, Americans again chose a warrior and man of action as its leader. Ulysses S. Grant had given the North what it desperately needed—victories. A beaten Confederate general had offered to negotiate a surrender only to be told: "No terms except an unconditional and immediate surrender can be accepted. I propose to move immediately upon your works." Grant's foe promptly turned over his sword in addition to his fourteen thousand men.

When critics bedeviled Grant, President Lincoln came to his general's defense. "I can't spare this man. He *fights*." Late in 1863, he was called to the capital, where Lincoln made him his commander in chief. Always his defender, Lincoln was said to have rebuked those who complained of Grant's heavy alcohol consumption. Find out what he drinks and give it to the other generals, the president told them.

Grant's many victories in the field made his presidency all but inevitable. As the man who'd accepted Robert E. Lee's surrender at Appomattox Courthouse in 1865, he was the hands-down Republican choice three years later. Tragically for his reputation, the eighteenth president really had neither a talent for governance nor the interest to serve as the country's chief executive.

Scandals dogged him, and as his poor appointments came back to haunt him, he found himself surrounded by the sleazier elements of the political world. To Grant's discredit, he would enter the history books as one of our very worst presidents.

Theodore Roosevelt

Generals Jackson, Harrison, and Grant were all just warm-up acts for the greatest man of action ever to be an American president. Teddy Roosevelt was a Dakota cowboy, a New York City police commissioner, a Rough Rider charging up San Juan Hill, and a big-game hunter.

He was also something never seen before in the White House—he was fun.

Both a showman and a show-off, he gave the American audience a one-man display of masculine adventurism such as they'd never seen before. Nor would they ever see its like again.

Mark Twain was characteristically clear-eyed about this combination of extreme energy and outlandish egoism. "Mr. Roosevelt," he wrote, "is the Tom Sawyer of the political world of the twentieth century; always showing off; always hunting for a chance to show off; in his frenzied imagination the Great Republic is a vast Barnum circus with him for a clown and the whole world for audience."

Roosevelt was utterly conscious of his own effect, however, and knew he was packaging himself for the consumption—and delight—of the American public. He felt strongly that the voters wanted from the man in the White House precisely what Lincoln had demanded of his generals—action.

"It is not the critic who counts," he said at the Sorbonne

during a 1910 tour, "not the man who points out how the strong man stumbles, or where the doer of deeds could have done them better. The credit belongs to the man who is actually in the arena, whose face is marred by dust and sweat and blood; who strives valiantly; who errs, and comes short again and again, because there is no effort without error and shortcoming; but who does actually strive to do the deeds."

But, like so many other Americans, Roosevelt had needed to reinvent himself before he would take center stage. Asthma and poor eyesight had been just two of the handicaps he'd struggled to overcome. Yet he never had motivation any greater than the punches he continually absorbed as a young man in the boxing ring. What was to be done, he wondered, about the way his opponents handled him with such "easy contempt?"

The solution he came up with was to join what he termed "the fellowship of the doers." That meant he would need to exercise twice as hard as he had before. No problem. He had the will and he had the energy, and he was giving notice that he, Theodore Roosevelt, was a man to be dealt with.

When the curtain rose on the career of Teddy Roosevelt, he stepped into the spotlight in the role of cowboy. It was as a rancher in the Dakotas—the rough-and-ready outdoorsman—that he first presented himself. The former sickly boy was now a buckaroo.

One favorite episode he liked to repeat was the story of his capture of three fugitives who had stolen a boat from the Roosevelt ranch. When he caught up with the trio, he pulled his gun and ordered them to put their hands up. "Finnegan hesitated for a second, his eyes fairly wolfish," Roosevelt wrote later, chronicling the episode for *Century* magazine. "Then, as I walked up within a few paces, covering the center of his chest so as to avoid overshooting, and repeating the command, he saw that he had no show, and, with an oath, let his rifle drop and held his hands up beside his head."

Next came the "Rough Riders." With America at war with Spain in 1898, Roosevelt assembled a motley crew of pals to ride with him into history. They included cowboys from his

Dakota days, a quartet of policemen who had served under him in New York City, a legendary Harvard quarterback, and, completing the ensemble, a renowned champion tennis player. To guard against the faint danger their efforts might escape attention, he signed with Scribner's to produce a war memoir to appear first in magazine form, later as "a permanent historical work." In his effort to grab the public imagination he was leaving nothing undone.

He wanted to be famous in 1898—and even more famous later.

The zenith of Teddy Roosevelt's adventures was the famous charge up Cuba's San Juan Hill. The chief Rough Rider had arrived in Cuba ready for action. When his orders came, he performed his self-styled war dance: "Shout hurrah for Erin Go Bragh! And all the Yankee nation!" His toast to victory in the upcoming battle was brimming with bravado. "To the officers—may they get killed, wounded or promoted."

Yet for all his shameless self-promotion, Teddy truly *was* a man of guts and action. And he figured America was ready for him.

Following his rousing exploits in Cuba, Roosevelt accepted the backing of New York State's Republican boss to run for governor. But he proved so independent that party leaders soon decided to get rid of this fellow they called "that damned cowboy."

Much like the backroom crowd that put Jefferson Smith in the U.S. Senate, the Republicans of New York miscalculated. Their solution was to gain for him the Republican nomination for vice president.

The ticket of President William McKinley and the hero of San Juan Hill was elected in 1900. Six months into the new term—September 6, 1901—McKinley fell to an assassin's bullet. Eight days later Theodore Roosevelt was sworn in as president.

TR proved to be as much of a "damned cowboy" in the White House as he'd been in New York. He enforced antitrust laws, fought for conservation, won approval of the Food and Drug bill, and moved to regulate the notoriously filthy meat-packing industry.

Not surprisingly, Teddy Roosevelt was the first president who understood how to manipulate the modern media. He created the institution now known as the White House press corps so he could have reporters on call when he had something to say. Those scribes who uncritically followed the White House line kept their access while those less inclined to TR worship didn't.

In 1912, when a gunman tried to kill him in Milwaukee, the force of the bullet was blunted by the manuscript of the day's speech and the iron spectacles case he carried in his chest pocket. The result was that the slug did not penetrate far into his chest. Bleeding, Teddy went ahead and gave the speech. "I do not care a rap about being shot," he declared with classic TR bravura.

Dwight D. Eisenhower

A West Point grad from Abilene, Kansas, Dwight David Eisenhower was a colonel when World War II began. Chosen to lead the invasion of North Africa in late 1942, he proved his ability to hold the allies together. In 1944, he directed the Allied invasion of Europe, again proving both his military and diplomatic skills.

With the war won, both the Democrats and the Republicans tried to recruit General Eisenhower, but he turned them down. While serving as president of Columbia University, he was appointed by President Harry Truman to be the supreme commander of the new North Atlantic Treaty Organization.

It was Senator Henry Cabot Lodge of Massachusetts who played the key role in getting Eisenhower to run for president. On a July tour of NATO headquarters in Paris, Lodge urged his World War II commander to run. When the five-star general refused, Lodge ignored him and took the plea public, proposing on *Meet the Press* that the country needed him.

In the subsequent months, a well-organized buildup would

bring the war commander into the fight for the Republican nomination. The "I like Ike" campaign would take the immensely popular war hero all the way to the White House.

Once in office, Eisenhower lived up to his campaign pledge to end the Korean War. While conservative on domestic issues, he continued the internationalist foreign policy of Roosevelt and Truman. A strong Cold Warrior, Ike spent eight years trying to limit the Soviet worldwide advance. He reigned over two terms of what he called "peace and prosperity," but by 1960, the American people were once again looking for a man of action. They would find him in a young World War II veteran who promised to "get this country moving again."

John F. Kennedy

It was 1946, and a young Jack Kennedy from Massachusetts was running for the House seat in Boston's eleventh Congressional District. Kennedy had served as a Navy lieutenant in the South Pacific during the war, where he was assigned to skipper a PT boat. While on a routine patrol mission, Kennedy's boat had been rammed by a Japanese destroyer and sliced in two.

The young Kennedy and most of his crew survived the initial impact, and Jack, as the ship's commanding officer, took responsibility for his men's well-being. They swam to a nearby island with Kennedy towing a burned crewman whose lifejacket he gripped with his teeth. After days of dodging the Japanese and scrounging for enough food and fresh water to stay alive, Kennedy and his men were rescued.

It was John Hersey's *New Yorker* article on Kennedy's ordeal, reprinted in *Reader's Digest,* that transformed this young veteran into a bona fide hero. When Kennedy's ambitious father, a ruthless self-made millionaire, used his Hollywood clout to get a newsreel produced narrating the tale of his son's wartime heroism, the boyishly handsome JFK became an instant celebrity.

"World War II was their greatest campaign manager," Kennedy campaign aide Billy Sutton would say of those politicians who were elected to Congress just back from the war.

But to the young Jack Kennedy, the time he'd spent in harm's way could not be counted in press clippings or even at the ballot box. He would confide later that, at the moment of his vessel's collision with the Japanese destroyer, he truly believed he was at the moment of his own death. It was as life-changing as only such instants can be, and the lasting effect of it was that he felt deeply bonded with other men of his generation who'd seen action in the South Pacific.

I firmly believe that as much as I was shaped by anything, so was I shaped by the hand of fate moving in World War II. Of course, the same can be said of almost any American or British or Australian man of my generation. The war made us. It was and is our single greatest moment. The memory of the war is a key to our characters. It serves as a breakwall between the indolence of our youths and earnestness of our manhoods. No school or parent could have shaped us the way that fight shaped us. No other experience could have brought forth in us the same fortitude and resilience. We were much shrewder and sadder when that long battle finally finished. The war made us get serious for the first time in our lives.

Whether or not the voters attached any deep significance to Kennedy's character-building World War II experience, it is clear that he himself did. He believed the war had "made" him, setting him down in a situation where he had either to act or die. However immature he had been—the Harvard-educated, playboy son of an autocratic father—before he shipped out, Jack Kennedy understood himself to be far different on his return.

It's hard not to agree with this assessment. The commander in chief who steered the country through the nuclear dread of the Cuban Missile Crisis was a grown-up version of the young skipper who got his crew home from the

Solomons. Whether the voters actually were able to sense this about their choice in 1960, they could see it in October 1962. Told he had to choose between Cold War appeasement and thermonuclear war, he refused to take the bait. He proved himself not just tougher than the Soviets, but shrewder than his generals.

CHAPTER 5

The Common Man

> For the first six months you'll wonder how the hell you got here, and after that you'll wonder how the hell the rest of us got here.
>
> SENATOR HAMILTON LEWIS OF ILLINOIS TO THE
> NEWLY ELECTED SENATOR HARRY TRUMAN OF
> MISSOURI, 1935

One of the notions we Americans hold dear is that the regular guy is just as good as the person born to privilege. In Europe, royalty makes for a great tourist attraction. Back in the United States, even homegrown snobs will agree that this is a country where, if you've got the stuff, you deserve a shot at showing it.

The movie *Dave* has a simple but very *American* plot. Dave Kovic, a small businessman who makes extra money as a presidential lookalike, gets recruited by the White House staff to serve as a decoy. The real chief executive, it seems, has a rather active libido. Our ringer's job is to be seen leaving a hotel so that the president, otherwise occupied, can linger longer and undetected.

The plot turns on the fate of the real president. Enjoying his young companion far too enthusiastically, he suffers a massive heart attack. Sadly for the White House staff, there's no way to explain how their man, seen leaving a hotel alive, should be discovered just hours later in that same hotel dead.

The only way, figures the conniving chief of staff, is to park Dave Kovic upstairs at the White House for the night.

It's the old twist, à la Mark Twain's *The Prince and the Pauper,* which is to say, the impersonator turns out to have a definite flair for the job.

But Dave needs help with the details. He calls in his accountant, Murray, from Baltimore. We see them sitting at a vast White House table with papers strewn all around them. There in front of them is a large leather volume labeled "Federal Budget."

MURRAY: I gotta tell ya, Dave. I've been going over this a bunch of times and a lot of this stuff doesn't add up. Who does these books?

DAVE: I'm not sure.

MURRAY: I just think they make this stuff a lot more complicated than it has to be.

DAVE: I'm not surprised. Can we save anywhere?

MURRAY: Well, yeah. But you gotta start making some choices.

DAVE: Choices?

MURRAY: You know—priorities. Remember when you couldn't get your car fixed 'cause you wanted to get that piano?

DAVE: You could buy it on payments.

MURRAY: Yeah. That's how you end up with a 400-billion-dollar deficit.

The fun of this scene lies in the premise. Rule-bound bureaucrats and overlobbied congressmen routinely fail, but a guy with simple math and common sense can figure it out. Want to house homeless children? Well then, hold off paying defense contractors until they've done the work. Want honest government? Put in honest people to do the job.

Americans are suspicious of elites, both social and intellectual. Save us from the know-it-alls and the think-they're-better-than us types. Let's find ourselves some *regular* people to run the country.

The Minutemen

Ever since 1776, this notion—that the common man can do the job—reliably pops up every four years. One could argue that it all started with those ordinary Americans in homespun clothes who stood up to the gaudily uniformed British troops at Lexington and Concord.

They were called Minutemen because they were citizens who vowed to be "ready in a minute's notice" to defend their communities and homes. Before dawn on April 19, 1775, a ragtag group of them assembled on Lexington Green to meet an advancing British force. There were only thirty-eight in all—barely enough to form one straight line across the green.

The standoff between the Minutemen and the British regulars that morning led to the famous "shot heard 'round the world." The American Revolution had begun.

No one knows who fired that first shot. According to the historian A. J. Langguth, most of the Minutemen did not fire until the battle had begun. Yet this did not stop the Redcoats from attacking. "At most," he writes, "a handful of . . . militia fired at the British, and that was only after the infantry was already pumping shot into the backs of fleeing Minutemen."

The Americans turned the tables down the road at Concord. At the Old North Bridge, the British had left only a few dozen men to guard the entrance to the town. The Minutemen force comprised, in Langguth's description, "four hundred grim farmers armed with muskets." Once again, there's disagreement over just who fired the first shot—but it didn't matter. This time, the Minutemen would rout the British, forcing them to break ranks and flee.

The disciplined British forces had better weapons and military training, but the Minutemen were fighting at home. It was where every hiding place was known to them. Practically invisible, they picked off the British soldiers as they marched on the road back to Boston. By day's end, the

British had seventy-three soldiers dead, 174 wounded. The Minutemen lost forty-nine, had thirty-nine wounded.

There is a great bronze statue at Old North Bridge outside of Concord. It stands across the creek from the spot where the Redcoats tried so desperately to defend their position. It is the figure of a Minuteman. He grips a plow in his left hand and a shotgun in his right. He is the reluctant warrior, but he is also the common man—these two powerful archetypes are at the heart of our national character, and it is impossible, over two hundred years later, to gaze upon the Minuteman without feeling moved.

The freedom of this country was won by its people. Any nation that owes its liberty to the courage and tenacity of its citizens forgets that at its peril.

Andrew Jackson

Just as Thomas Jefferson had bestowed his vision on his nation as it sought to free itself from foreign rule, so Andrew Jackson himself came to embody that vision once independence had been won.

After taking the oath in 1829 and delivering one of the shortest inaugural addresses ever, Jackson, a man of little formal education, walked down Pennsylvania Avenue, inviting the entire crowd along the way to join him at the White House. The First Family's home filled with hordes of people,

and china and glassware were broken in the excitement. People left only when they learned that refreshments were being served out on the lawn. Jackson himself had to escape the commotion through a back door.

According to the Jackson biographer Arthur Schlesinger, Jr., the scene prompted Daniel Webster to note sarcastically that "the shouting crowd on Inauguration Day . . . really seemed to think the country is rescued from some dreadful danger."

While some looked on in horror, others proclaimed it a victory for the common man. "It was a proud day for the people," wrote the *Argus of Western America,* "General Jackson is their own president." It called the new president "plain in his dress, unaffected and familiar in his manners," and a "hero of a popular triumph." The backcountry folk had already been on his side; now the rest of the American citizenry was seeing what sturdy, plain cloth he was made of.

Jackson went on to give federal jobs to two thousand of his supporters. Government positions should be kept "so plain and simple," he said, that any qualified applicant could fill them on a rotating basis.

His election enlivened the nation. The political establishment had been put on notice.

Abraham Lincoln

Is there anyone who doesn't know Abraham Lincoln was born in a log cabin? He spent his youth and young adulthood on the verge of poverty because his family, like so many settlers on the western frontier of the era, was perpetually starting all over again.

School was a luxury. At one point, the tall, strong young man hired himself out to split rails for neighbors' fences, and for a time he was nicknamed "the Rail-splitter." But he is more widely known as "Honest Abe," for his determination to pay off every debt in the face of even the worst setback.

Despite his lack of a fancy education, Lincoln would be the most *eloquent* man ever to serve as president. His Gettysburg Address was a mere 268 words. Yet they are among the most unforgettable ever spoken. He proclaimed that the

Union must be saved and urged those attending to resolve
that the battle dead buried beneath them "shall not have died
in vain—that this nation, under God, shall have a new birth
of freedom, and that government of the people, by the people, for the people, shall not perish from the earth."

In his Second Inaugural Address, perhaps the most magnificent speech ever given in this country, Lincoln saw bibli-
cal meaning in the horror of the great Civil War:

> The Almighty has his own purposes. "Woe unto the world be-
> cause of offences! for it must needs be that offences come; but
> woe to that man by whom the offence cometh!" If we shall sup-
> pose that American Slavery is one of those offences which, in
> the providence of God, must needs come, but which, having
> continued through His appointed time, He now wills to remove,
> and that He gives to both North and South, this terrible war, as
> the woe due to those by whom the offence came, shall we dis-
> cern therein any departure from those divine attributes which the
> believers in a Living God always ascribe to Him? Fondly do we
> hope—fervently do we pray—that this mighty scourge of war
> may speedily pass away. Yet, if God wills that it continue, until
> all the wealth piled by the bond-man's two hundred and fifty
> years of unrequited toil shall be sunk, and until every drop of
> blood drawn with the lash, shall be paid by another drawn with
> the sword, as was said three thousand years ago, so still it must

be said "the judgments of the Lord, are true and righteous alto-gether."

Born a common man, he had an uncommon vision of his country's destiny. To Lincoln, the survival of the world's only country committed to democratic society was para-mount. It was his central belief in the cause—saving the union he believed to be "the last, best hope of earth"—that gave his leadership in the time of this country's worst crisis its eternal power.

Harry S Truman

Americans like to hope that a president, tested, rises to the office. If we elect him, he will do the job as it should be done. Harry Truman, who became president upon the death of Franklin Delano Roosevelt just weeks before the final de-feat of Germany in World War II, is the most splendid exam-ple of this.

Sworn in as vice president just three months earlier, Tru-man had never expected to go so far in life. He hardly knew FDR at all and had been selected to run with him in 1944 as a safe choice over the left-leaning incumbent vice president, Henry Wallace. He had scant contact with the president dur-ing the brief time they served together. When he got word

that Roosevelt was dead, he was stunned. "I felt like the moon, the stars, and all the planets had fallen on me," he would confess later.

"He was not a hero or a magician or a chess player or an

obsessive," Mary McGrory wrote upon Truman's own death. "He was a certifiable member of the human race, direct, fallible, and unexpectedly wise when it counted."

Yes, he was. Forced with the unimaginably difficult decision whether to use the newly developed atom bomb to end the war with Japan and therefore avoid a million American casualties in an invasion, Truman gave the go-ahead. When the Soviet dictator Josef Stalin nearly succeeded in bringing Greece and Turkey into his sphere, Truman immediately sent aid to the two vulnerable countries.

Thus was born the "Truman Doctrine." That same year, 1947, he fought to win congressional approval for an ambitious blueprint to rebuild Western Europe. The Marshall Plan was the perfect Cold War action, its premise the idea that an economically strong Europe could more easily withstand the lure of communism. Ultimately, thanks to the Marshall Plan, a standard of freedom and comfort was set that made the captive nations of Eastern Europe more aware of their deficiencies.

There was little in Truman's background to suggest he could ever emerge a leader of vision. When he heard that he was being proposed as a senate candidate in 1934, he couldn't sleep that night he was so overwhelmed. "I thought two weeks ago that retirement on a virtual pension in some minor county office was all that was in store for me."

He had never gone to college and had failed at business

upon returning from World War I. But in Washington, he got reassurance: "Harry, don't start out with an inferiority complex," Senator Hamilton Lewis of Illinois, the number two Democratic leader, said one day after taking a seat next to him. "For the first six months you'll wonder how the hell you got here, and after that you'll wonder how the hell the rest of us got here."

Truman never did learn how to spell. Occasion was "occation." Senator Byrnes was "Senator Burns." "Hawaii" was hopeless. He couldn't even spell the name of the street he lived on in Independence, Missouri. It was forever "Deleware" Street to him.

But he remembered names. He remembered what the real people he knew cared about, what their kids were doing in life, to whom they were related. He came across as the man he really was—a regular fellow who just as easily could be standing behind the counter when you went to buy a new pair of socks. Yet, from the moment he took the oath of office, this owlish little country gentleman with the thick glasses and high, flat voice had the power of life and death in his hands.

The important thing is how Harry Truman always, as president, had the guts to do what he thought was right. When Moscow closed off Berlin in 1948, he created the "airlift" that saved the city. When North Korea invaded South Korea, he backed a United Nations campaign to resist and throw back the invaders. It was an unpopular war, but he knew he had to fight it.

The result was, when he left office, he had a dismal Gallup Poll job approval of 23 percent. Tough decisions don't always make friends.

That judgment would change in time. Today Harry Truman stands as one of the great presidents. He is hugely respected both among Democrats and their opposite numbers. In fact, he is hands down every rock-ribbed Republican's favorite Democrat of the twentieth century.

The biographer David McCullough has captured Truman best: "He was the kind of president the founding fathers had in mind for the country. He came directly from the people. He was America." Senator Adlai Stevenson III, son of the two-time Democratic presidential candidate, called Truman "an object lesson in the vitality of popular government; an example of the ability of this society to yield up, from the most unremarkable origins, the most remarkable men."

The Appeal of the "Common Man"

The innate resourcefulness of the little guy is the irresistible notion behind such movies as *Mr. Smith Goes to Washington* and *Dave*. Even though he's put in the White House as an impostor, Dave does the right thing. He proposes legislation to ensure that every American is guaranteed a chance to work. Dave also wins our heart by having the guts to fire the White House chief of staff who gave him the outrageously illegal gig in the first place—impersonating the real president who's being kept in a vegetative state somewhere in the bowels of the executive mansion's basement.

It's a fantasy of the most delightful sort, especially for us political junkies.

"America has been very busy the last couple of centuries developing a strange and complex notion about its ideal," the film historian Donald Spoto has written, "someone called the Common Man." He's talking about Rick Blaine, Jeff Smith, Dave Kovic, Harry Truman. "You know who this common man is: the ordinary guy next door. He's patriotic and idealistic, but not heroic, unless he's pushed too far, and then heroism is usually an accident."

When an imaginative and—let's face it—patriotic Hollywood scriptwriter puts his own spin on the glorious ordinariness of the common man risen to the occasion, this is what we get:

DAVE: See, there are certain things you should expect from a president. I ought to care more about you than I do about me . . . I ought to care more about what's right than I do about what's popular . . . I ought to be willing to give this whole thing up for something I believe in . . .

This is exactly—*exactly*—what the American public wants from its presidents, even if we've somehow managed to keep our expectations lowered.

The thought that a "common man" might be found to lead the country was very much alive in 2000. But there wasn't one running. Vice President Al Gore had traveled the world, hung out with leaders from Tabo Mbeki to Hosni Mubarak. During the course of the presidential debates he even invoked the name of the health minister of Ghana.

But a presidential election is not a matter of international name-dropping any more than it's a spelling bee (lucky for Truman!). For the American people, it's a matter of which candidate they feel more comfortable with, more connected to. Gore had the issues down pat and George W. Bush often floundered. One knew a lot, the other knew enough.

So who did we want?

It turned out not to be a contest of credentials. Had it been, Al Gore would have cleaned Bush's clock and be halfway through his first term. But he couldn't convince anyone anywhere that he was a regular guy. A plurality of people voted for him. Most voters just didn't want to hang out with him for four years.

CHAPTER 6

Underdogs

David is still getting good PR for beating Goliath.

REPUBLICAN POLITICAL STRATEGIST

LEE ATWATER

*R*ocky took America by storm in the late autumn of 1976. It's the story of a thirty-year-old "bum" from Philadelphia who gets a once-in-a-lifetime shot at greatness. At theaters across the country, audiences stood up as it ended—many with tears in their eyes—and applauded, helping this underdog of a movie become one of the most successful films of all time.

The tag line in the ad campaign for *Rocky*—"His whole life was a million-to-one shot"—echoes the biography of its star, Sylvester Stallone. Before he wrote the screenplay in three days, this underemployed young actor had submitted thirty-two scripts to Hollywood producers without a single green light. This did not keep the unknown Stallone from demanding the right to play the title role.

127

The plot of *Rocky* is basic. But that's all that's necessary. A has-been Philadelphia boxer, Rocky Balboa, gets an opportunity out of nowhere. The World Heavyweight Champion, Apollo Creed, has come to town for a heavily hyped bout with a serious contender. But a training accident has scratched his rival from the card. With the arena rented and the date scheduled, the promoters decide to cut their losses by giving a local guy a shot at the title.

Even before the opening credits are finished, we have seen that Rocky is anything but heroic. Living in a one-room dump in North Philly, he's an over-the-hill palooka who makes his living as a soft-hearted enforcer for the local "numbers" rackets.

The movie magic comes when he begins to transform himself into someone who can be a contender.

Flash forward to the fifteenth round. Rocky, barely conscious after the beating he has taken, begs his manager to open up his swollen eye so he can see enough to finish the fight.

"Cut me!" he demands.

In the other corner, the champion is so angry at his humiliating inability to pummel this nobody into submission that he refuses to let the fight be declared a technical knockout owing to the other man's condition.

"You ain't stoppin' nothin', man," he sneers at his cornerman.

At the final bell, both boxers are wrecked, able to do nothing but hang on to each other. The judges rule a split decision: two votes for the champion, one for the challenger. Rocky Balboa is no longer a "bum" but a hero who, on one unforgettable night in his hometown, took on the champion of the world and gave him a fight.

As Sylvester Stallone explained "when they're cheering for Rocky, they're cheering for themselves." This is a country that has become used to winning, but remains emotionally invested in the underdog.

Back in the very beginning, the United States itself was a longshot. In 1778, the British forces included fifty thousand regular troops and more than thirty thousand German mercenaries. George Washington never had more than twenty thousand men under his command.

Yet we won. Here we are to prove it.

The secret is that, though the Royal army won battle after battle, the Americans never really lost. The rebels kept coming at them, bolstered by their countrymen's fervor and relying on savvy back-country stratagems learned during the French and Indian War.

Today, remembering its own origins, if only subconsciously, America continues its romance with the underdog, its infatuation with the guy who's not supposed to win.

Rumble in the Jungle

In 1974, Muhammad Ali was supposed to be killed by George Foreman at four o'clock in the morning, Zaire time. The fighter who once bragged he could "float like a butterfly and sting like a bee" was now a decade older and facing a fighter whose punches were stronger and faster.

But let's go back a little further: when Cassius Clay fought the ex-convict Sonny Liston, then heavyweight champion, nobody thought Liston had anything to worry about from this Louisville kid who'd won in the Olympics. No one so far had even given Liston a fight, certainly not Floyd Patterson, the champ he'd demolished to gain the title.

Before facing Clay, Liston issued the usual blustering pre-fight threats. In fact, reported fight buff George Plimpton, "public sentiment was for Liston, a Mob-controlled thug, to take care of the lippy upstart. Liston concurred, saying he was going to put his fist so far down his opponent's throat, he was going to have trouble removing it."

But the kid won and changed the world of boxing. He also changed his name. Joining the Nation of Islam, he became Muhammad Ali. When people criticized this decision, he retorted, "I don't have to be what you want me to be; I'm free to be what I want."

In 1967, he rebelled again, refusing to accept induction into the U.S. Army. "I ain't got no quarrel with them Viet-

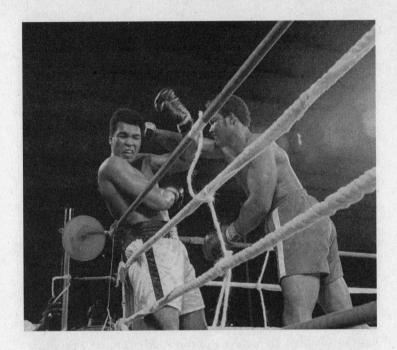

cong," he said, and declared that his Muslim religion taught him that the fighting in Vietnam was immoral. Charged with draft evasion, he lost his boxing title.

For more than three years, at the peak of his boxing fitness, he was prevented by the government from fighting. Yet when a Russian reporter goaded him with questions about the plight of American blacks, Ali refused to allow himself to be exploited. "Man, the USA is the best country in the world, counting yours."

When the Supreme Court ruled in Ali's favor, allowing him to fight again, he faced the new champ Joe Frazier, and lost. Meanwhile a ferocious George Foreman knocked out Frazier in two rounds. Ali went up against Frazier for the second time in early 1974. This time he won, gaining the right to face Foreman for the championship later that year. Yet no one who cared about boxing could take any joy in an Ali-Foreman match-up.

Thanks to the documentary *When We Were Kings,* we have a stirring record of that historic Foreman-Ali fight.

In it, Ali appears to approach the fight with characteristic braggadocio, yet something is odd about the way he's training. Norman Mailer, whose commentary is heard in *When We Were Kings,* paid notice: "He would go against the rope and he would let people punch him, very heavy hitters who were sort of clumsy. He'd let them bang away at him. It was as if he wanted to train his body to receive this message of punishment."

In the first round, Ali went on the attack, trying to knock out the larger, stronger Foreman. Not a smart move. "He was in the ring with a man he could not dominate, who was stronger than him, who was not afraid of him, who was gonna try to knock him out, and who punched harder than Ali could punch," Mailer recalled. "Ali had a look on his face that I'll never forget. It was the only time that I ever saw *fear* in Ali's eyes."

But as the rounds wore on, with the contender on the ropes and the champ pounding away, Foreman became more and more tired. In the fifth, Ali began to attack, landing solid punches to Foreman's head. Foreman's arms were too tired to block the punches. By round eight, Ali was landing hard rights on Foreman. After three connected, Ali fired a right at his opponent's jaw that sent Foreman to the floor and kept him there for the 10-count.

The "Rumble in the Jungle" turned Muhammad Ali into a national icon. Even those who hated his name change, questioned his religious conversion, and condemned his refusal to join the army knew they had seen something truly transcendent. A man of lesser power had beaten his terrifying rival using his wits, his guile, and his guts.

Oprah Winfrey

She was born in segregated Mississippi to unmarried parents and raised dirt poor by her grandmother. Today, Oprah Winfrey is one of the most influential women in America.

According to her biographer George Mair, Oprah's poor Mississippi childhood with her grandmother was "a solitary routine filled with daily farm chores . . . without playmates, television, or toys except for a corncob doll." Her mother worked as a maid far away in Milwaukee, and had trouble making ends meet. Later, after moving to be with her mother, Oprah lived in tight quarters, sharing a cramped two-bedroom apartment in Milwaukee with her mother, half-siblings, and other relatives.

As Oprah grew older, her life did not get better. Terrible things happened: She was raped by an older male relative. She struggled in school, and rebelled at home. Her mother tried to force her into a home for wayward teens. Finally, Oprah was sent to Nashville to live with her father.

Her years in Nashville made the difference. A lonely child who'd spent a lot of time reading and educating herself, she now gained enough confidence to enter a few local beauty contests, including one that won her a scholarship to Tennessee State University. She also landed a radio station job reading the news. By the end of her sophomore year at TSU, she had been hired as Nashville's first black female television news anchor.

Winfrey's next move was to Baltimore, where she anchored the six o'clock news on television. Next came a job in Chicago, where she hosted a morning program called *A.M. Chicago.* Before long it was renamed *The Oprah Winfrey Show.* In 1986, it went national.

Once *The Oprah Winfrey Show* entered national syndication, it took off. Its star became a household name around the globe. She has parlayed her success into a half-billion-dollar enterprise. She was named to *Time*'s list of the hundred most important people of the century. Yet she has remained in her heart the girl whose chances for such glory were hardly assured. Never doubting her own abilities or doing anything other than exulting in her own triumphs, she nonetheless knows exactly how she's linked to her millions of viewers.

"The reason I communicate with all these people is because I think I'm every woman and I've had every malady and I've been on every diet and I've had men who have done me wrong, honey. So I related to all of that. And I'm not afraid or ashamed to say it," Winfrey once explained.

"What I'm trying to do with the show," she told another questioner, "is to get people to see where they are stuck and be able to live up to whatever is their human potential."

Winfrey understands brilliantly the power she possesses. Her intelligence, along with her compassion, has made her brand of television the gold standard.

Even the men running for president of the United States in 2000 couldn't avoid her. Both showed up in her studio, and it's arguable that Bush's appearance boosted him in the polls.

"Like many, many memorable guests before him, Bush cried on *The Oprah Winfrey Show*. Talking about when his wife Laura became toxemic while carrying their twins, his eyes became wet and continued to glisten even after the following commercial break. And so, if Al Gore went on *Oprah* last week to prove he was a real person," wrote *Salon*'s David Skinner, "George W. Bush proved he was a real *Oprah* guest, which is even better."

This is Winfrey's great discovery about America. A country that loves to win has, to its great moral credit, never stopped rooting for the underdog. As that canny Republican campaign strategist, the late Lee Atwater, once noted, "David is still getting good PR for beating Goliath."

CHAPTER 7

The Lone Hero

Injun will chase a thing till he thinks he's chased it
enough. Then he quits. Same way when he runs.
Seems like he never learns there's such a thing as a
critter who'll just keep comin'.

ETHAN EDWARDS, THE SEARCHERS

Amerca doesn't *fit in* with other countries. In good
times, we like to go it our own way. But even when we join
the posse—think of World War II and the Persian Gulf campaign—we want to do it on our own terms. We're willing to
take on sidekicks as long as we get to be the trail boss.

This first-among-equals mentality of ours may explain the
strange kind of hero we tend to celebrate. He's almost never
what you'd call "one of the boys." More often he's a loner
who arrives out of nowhere, saves the day, then disappears
again over the horizon. While he may have a mysterious or
even dark past, he comes equipped with the courage and generosity to do what other men can't.

Yet he's the hero or *nothing*. No other role would suit him.

The Searchers

John Ford's *The Searchers,* I think—and I'm hardly alone in this—is the best Western ever made. It's a story that cuts close to the American bone, revealing to us the kind of dark hero that we are drawn to again and again. These are men who reflect back at us the shocking hardness buried deep in our own souls.

In *The Searchers,* John Wayne plays the Texan Ethan Edwards, a rough-hewn fellow who's fought on the losing side of the Civil War. Returning to his brother's ranch, he soon joins a party of local ranchers lured from the homestead to chase Comanche cattle rustlers.

The next scene, after Ethan and the others ride off, is as close to being both nightmare and reality as you're likely to encounter in a lifetime of movie going. As night falls, Ethan's brother realizes too late that the cattle rustling was just a ruse that would leave his family unprotected. In the approaching darkness, he, his wife, and two daughters can hear the Comanches signaling to each other—and know that they are doomed.

When Ethan arrives back at his brother's ranch, he finds his beloved sister-in-law raped and murdered, and his brother dead. But that is not all: his two nieces are missing.

Ethan immediately joins the posse formed to bring back

the abducted girls. When the other men fall back, reluctant to carry on, Ethan becomes ignited by the obsession to continue the hunt.

For five years, Ethan chases down every clue to his kidnapped nieces. At first he wants to save them. Then he finds the ravaged body of the older girl, and he realizes they have reached the age to be taken sexually. Ethan learns that the surviving girl, Debbie (played by a young Natalie Wood), has been assimilated into Indian society, and it becomes unclear whether he wants to rescue her or kill her.

What's at stake now is the honor of his tribe, and Ethan is just the man to uphold it. A white man who knows how to scalp an Indian, he intends to turn the tables of terror. His relentless pursuit makes him more than human: he is the dark side of the noble frontiersman, he is the cowboy as avenging demon. Ethan will make the Comanches he's chasing fear him not just because he will kill them in this world, but because he will damn them in the next as well. He does so by shooting out the eyes of a dead brave whose grave he uncovers, thereby mutilating him beyond deliverance.

"We'll find 'em in the end, I promise you," Ethan says when his companion suggests giving up their grim quest. "We'll find 'em, just as sure as the turnin' of the earth."

It is this unflinching commitment, fueled by the most primordial power, that grips us as we study our relentless hero.

He is loyal to a tribe from which he himself stays apart. There's something unholy about him—but also something pure.

Like Ethan Edwards, America itself has a shadowed past. The people who came here wanted land and took it from those who were here already. They used slave labor, importing men, women, whole families from Africa to do the work of growing tobacco and cotton. Those slaves were forced out to the fields with the whip and threat of worse.

It is not a pretty history. Yet it is ours.

Even today, despite our vast power in the world, America remains a misfit nation. We are not European. We are not really part of the Americas to our south, nor do we have the easy kinship with Canada that a common language and British heritage would suggest. We don't really fit in anywhere.

This explains our fascination with outsiders. The hero who lives his life without checking the polls is the one we will always prefer.

The Searchers is about a man who has lived his life apart and will end his days that way. This is the role *America* plays in the world. We are a country that must live with the fact that we wiped out Indians and enslaved Africans. Yet we are the country that gallops in to save the day when it really matters. Casually dismissed by some of the older, more arrogant nations of Europe as crude and callow, we arrived like the cavalry to save the day in two world wars, and more recently in Bosnia, Kosovo, and every trouble spot brought to a boil by the old order.

The Last of the Mohicans and Daniel Boone

One of America's earliest lone heroes, Hawkeye, made his appearance in James Fenimore Cooper's *The Last of the Mohicans*. With the same bloodlines as Ethan Edwards, he carried the spirit of pioneer America. Like Edwards, he knew the ways of the Indian, but unlike him, he respected him and his beliefs. It was the Indian, after all, who taught him to live in the wilderness, to survive its dangers. "God made us all, white, black and red, and, no doubt, had his own wise intentions in colouring us differently."

It is the 1750s, and the French and Indian War is raging. Hawkeye has taken upon himself the duty to protect two young women on their way to the besieged Fort William Henry to visit their father, the fort's commander. We see that he is a man who lives by his own rules, a code he has fashioned on the frontier. Though he lives a quarter of a century before the Revolution, he is, in character and attitude, already an American.

Indeed, Cooper's hero is a buckskinned brother to the men

who would write the rules for a new country, pen that Declaration which would include the right to pursue happiness, give us that Constitution establishing evenhanded justice.

And it is for those high standards that Hawkeye fights. "For whatever traits the Western Hero is admired, and for whatever values his world is cherished," Warren Walker has written in an essay on Hawkeye and the American West, "his story endures as a synthesis of past and present, of fact and fiction, of the written and oral traditions. For better or for worse, he has emerged as the culture hero of America."

"Hawkeye's frontier spirit, his love of the wilderness, his relations with Indians, with women, with the English—all become resources for picturing our own lives. But not directly," write Martin Barker and Roger Sabin in their book *The Lasting of the Mohicans*. "For example, the 'English' in the story won't literally represent English people." Instead, they can be seen as any elite ruling clique that presumes in both attitude and behavior to govern society due to birth or social rank.

While the "English" clearly represent the ruling elite, in the same sense, Hawkeye is clearly one of us. Two decades before the Revolution we see him confront the English and dictate his own course for the new land. His strengths are his marksmanship and his honesty. They are the arms he uses to defeat both the Indians and the English. They are the engine and the compass of the new country that he champions by his very being.

Looking back at him, we can see that Hawkeye personified the youth and spirit of a country that was only beginning to reveal itself.

James Fenimore Cooper admitted that the hero of *The Last of the Mohicans* was inspired by the authentic American hero, Daniel Boone.

In 1773, Indians attacked Boone and a large group of settlers attempting to pass through the Cumberland Gap. Boone lost his son, James, in the attack, and the surviving settlers decided to turn back. The trip was a failure, but Boone would not accept defeat. He would return to the frontier continually, eventually making it his home.

Two years later, Boone trailblazed a path through the Cumberland Gap that eased the strain of travel from the east to the west side of the Appalachians, opening the frontier to thousands. After completing the Wilderness Road, he built a fort at Boonesborough, where he settled with his family. It was three years later that Cherokees kidnapped Boone's daughter Jemima while she was canoeing on the Kentucky River. The frontiersman successfully led a rescue party to free Jemima and two other girls.

The Last of the Mohicans was written at a time when America was divided between the established East and the untamed frontier. People living in the "West"—Kentucky, Tennessee—resented the Eastern banks that controlled their money and the Washington politicians who tried to control them. They resented the social elite of the big cities for looking down on them, in effect becoming the new "English." To the man on the frontier, the Easterner was a "dude," an overdressed, overeducated man of the office and the city.

The Turner Thesis

In 1890, the historian Frederick Jackson Turner published a thesis about the power and allure of the western frontier. As long as America was expanding westward, he maintained, there would always be a part of the country living in less developed circumstances.

This "return to primitive conditions on a continually advancing frontier," he wrote, worked a powerful influence on the country as a whole. "This perennial rebirth, this fluidity of American life, this expansion westward with its new opportunities, its continuous touch with the simplicity of primitive society, furnish the forces dominating American character."

Turner saw this as a gradual process that was neither Indian nor European—it was uniquely *American.*

The frontier is the line of most rapid and effective Americanization. The wilderness masters the colonist. It finds him a European in dress, industries, tools, modes of travel, and thought. It takes him from the railroad car and puts him in the birch canoe. It strips off the garments of civilization and arrays him in the hunting shirt and the moccasin. It puts him in the log cabin of the Cherokee and Iroquois and runs an Indian palisade around him. Before long he has gone to planting Indian corn and plowing with a sharp stick, he shouts the war cry and takes the scalp in orthodox Indian fashion. In short, at the frontier the environment is at first too strong for the man. He must accept the conditions which it furnishes, or perish, and so he fits himself into the Indian clearings and follows the Indian trails. Little by little he transforms the wilderness, but the outcome is not the old Europe, not simply the development of Germanic germs, any more than the first phenomenon was a case of reversion to the Germanic mark. The fact is, that here is a new product that is American.

At first, the frontier was the Atlantic coast. It was the frontier of Europe in a very real sense. Moving westward, the frontier became more and more American. Each new frontier leaves its traces behind it, and when it becomes a settled area the region still partakes of the frontier characteristics. Thus the advance of the frontier has meant a steady movement away from the influence of Europe, a steady growth of independence on American lines. And to study this advance, the men who grew up under these conditions, and the political, economic, and social results of it, is to study the really American part of our history. . . .

Turner argued that the frontier created a "new order" where "immigrants were Americanized, liberated, and fused into a mixed race, English in neither nationality nor characteristics."

Steadily the frontier of settlement advanced and carried with it individualism, democracy, and nationalism, and powerfully affected the East and the Old World. The result is that to the frontier the American intellect owes its striking characteristics. That coarseness and strength combined with acuteness and inquisitiveness; that practical, inventive turn of mind, quick to find expedients; that masterful grasp of material things, lacking in the artistic but powerful to effect great ends; that restless, nervous energy; that dominant individualism, working for good and for evil, and withal that buoyancy and exuberance which comes with freedom—these are traits of the frontier.

Turner presents a romanticized picture of the frontier and its effect on our character. I would carry his argument further. Through the eighteenth century and all but a decade of the nineteenth Americans lived at the edge of a wild, uncivilized western territory.

But that wasn't the end of its influence.

Through the entire twentieth century, we Americans celebrated that frontier life in film and fiction with a reverence approaching ancestor worship. Every young boy from Brooklyn to Beverly Hills wore cowboy clothes and imagined owning a pony. The thrill of the American West—enshrined by Remington's bronzes, Zane Grey's pulp novels and John Ford's movies—remains our nation's great collective memory. Lonely on the range, the cowboy remains a robust American archetype.

Travis Bickel

Twenty years after *The Searchers* came Martin Scorsese's *Taxi Driver.* Its hero Travis Bickel is an angry outcast, a Viet-

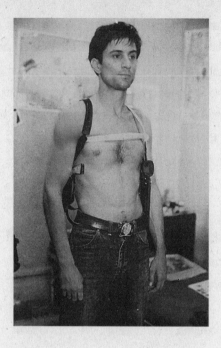

nam veteran, a human time bomb who becomes obsessed with saving a young teenage runaway.

Bickel, who drives a cab at night in New York, is a modern-day Ethan Edwards. (The screenwriter, Paul Schrader, admitted as much.) Like that veteran of an earlier lost-cause war, he has a flawed but faithful heart. He wants to find the young teenager, played by Jodie Foster, who has fled her family to sell her body on the mean streets. Bickel, alone, is determined to save her.

In the terrifying buildup to the film's climax, our hero

turns and glares at himself in the mirror to then recite conversations in which he challenges imaginary enemies, rehearsing his gunslinger's quick draw: "You talkin' to me? You talkin' to me? You talkin' to me?" In an urban jungle where even eye contact can be deadly, Travis Bickel will dare the predator he stalks to not avert his glance.

Against the backdrop of an urban hell, we are watching a disquieting but oddly comforting figure from our frontier past. If we cannot clap at Travis Bickel's hair-trigger violence, we still are drawn hypnotically to his edgy generosity, his readiness to give all in the struggle that decent folk have too easily abandoned.

Shane

George Stevens's *Shane,* another Western classic, has a storyline straight out of Frederick Jackson Turner.

A lone gunslinger arrives one day at a Wyoming homestead. Like *The Searchers,* it's the story of a stranger who shows up in the nick of time. Shane—the only name he's known by—sides with the farmers against the big rancher, a tyrant bent on running them off land he considers his own.

We first meet Shane as he rides in from nowhere. He is obviously a man with a past. When questioned merely out of friendly curiosity, he isn't forthcoming.

STARRETT: I wouldn't ask you where you're bound.

SHANE: One place or another, some place I've never been.

Joe Starrett hires Shane to live and work with him. Shane trades in his gun and buckskins for the quiet life, only to find himself embroiled in a range war. Rufe Ryker, a cattle baron intent on regaining his grazing land, harasses the homesteaders. But led by Starrett, they refuse to quit.

The gun battle between Shane and Jack Wilson, the villainous gunslinger hired by Ryker—the movie's high point—is one of Hollywood's great scenes. It also says a helluva lot about how we Americans view good and evil. A Joe Starrett can farm the land, even lead his community. But the reason we cheer Shane and fear for his survival is because we know how much we need men like him. It takes a hardened outrider to clear the trail of reptiles like Wilson.

In all these stories from *Casablanca* to *Shane,* we understand intuitively that once these heroes have taken up our cause, they are destined to leave us. Just as Rick Blaine's power lies in his sacrifice, so does Shane's.

"I gotta be goin' on . . . Joey, there's no living with, with a killing. There's no going back from it. Right or wrong, it's a brand, a brand that sticks. There's no going back." This is what he tells Starrett's young son, who idolizes him.

When he's among us, this man of dark pedigree can show a courage and commitment beyond that of ordinary mortals.

What we don't know about him becomes irrelevant. His courage and the gift he makes to us—as generous as it is dangerous for him to make—overwhelm us. This is the figure we Americans cherish. Could his be the role we want our country to play?

CHAPTER 8

Pioneers

What do you say? Let's try it!

CHARLES LINDBERGH, 7:51 A.M., MAY 20, 1927

John F. Kennedy grasped beautifully the notion of the frontier. The author of *Profiles in Courage* understood our love of the pathfinder, the leader so at ease in the world that as each grand new territory opened before him it quickly became his own. JFK challenged a generation that had fought alongside him in World War II to join him in facing a "New Frontier," enshrining the phrase in our political lexicon.

"Today some would say that those struggles are all over— that all the horizons have been explored, that all the battles have been won, that there is no longer an American frontier," he said in accepting the 1960 Democratic nomination in Los Angeles. "No one in this vast assemblage will agree with those sentiments. For the problems are not all solved and the battles are not all won, and we stand today on the edge of a New Frontier—the frontier of the 1960s—a frontier of unknown opportunities and perils, a frontier of unfulfilled hopes and threats."

Kennedy knew America: "What I see is a country which finds its happiness in moving forward." Just as we love men of action, we crave for the country itself to be on the move. Like a boat in a fast current we are a country that drifts when the engine's turned off—and Americans don't like the feeling.

Let's "get this country moving again," he said. And America was thrilled, a little nervous, but thrilled, definitely, all the same.

Our readiness to pull up stakes and head out for the new territories is as deep in our dreams as in Huck Finn's. We are, for all our faults, an adventurous people. I think it explains why we celebrate those who lead the way. A country that always wants to move forward has an especially high regard for the scouts sent out to mark the trail.

Daniel Boone and the Western Frontier

Daniel Boone was the prototype for every Westerner, from James Fenimore Cooper's Hawkeye to the many John Ford heroes. "It was too crowded back East," Boone explained in what would today be a perfect sound bite. "I had to have more elbow-room."

This desire to see and experience the wide open spaces for oneself was captured by Mark Twain in *The Adventures of Huckleberry Finn.* "I reckon I got to light out for the territory ahead of the rest," Huck says at the end. "Because Aunt Sally she's going to adopt me and civilize me and I can't stand it. I been there before."

It's the same freedom-loving zest we catch in the step of Rick Blaine at the end of *Casablanca* when he heads off with his friend Captain Renault to that "Free French garrison at Brazzaville."

This vision of America chasing the horizon started with Daniel Boone. "With his native capacity for leadership and decision, his enduring tranquility despite setbacks, his love of hunting, trapping, and the outdoors, he was one of the great un-machined men of our frontier days," writes the biographer Marshall Fishwick.

"Possessing a body at once powerful, compact, and capable of tremendous activity and resistance when roused, a clear eye and a deadly aim, taciturn in his demeanor, symmetrical and instinctive in understanding, Boone stood for his race, the affirmation of that wild logic, which in times past had mastered another wilderness and now, renascent, would master this, to prove it potent."

Daniel Boone offered the folks around him a role model, the men and women back east a native hero. His story gave the country a fresh lore to go with its expanding frontier.

Frederick Jackson Turner was the first writer to recognize the power of the frontier in the American mind. "Western democracy has been from the time of its birth idealistic. The very fact of the wilderness appealed to men as a fair, blank page on which to write a new chapter in the story of man's struggle for a higher type of society. The Western wilds, from the Alleghenies to the Pacific, constituted the richest free gift that was ever spread out before civilized man. To the peasant and artisan of the Old World, bound by the chains of social class, as old as custom and as inevitable as fate, the West offered an exit into a free life and greater well-being . . . and . . . the chance for indefinite ascent in the scale of social advance."

Charles Lindbergh

On Friday, May 20, 1927, at 7:52 in the morning, a young man took off in the monoplane *The Spirit of St. Louis* from Long Island, New York. Thirty-three hours later, he landed at Le Bourget airport in Paris. As he began to descend he could see a long line of traffic headed for the field to see the first man ever to fly across the Atlantic Ocean.

From the moment he touched down, Charles A. Lindbergh

became a greater figure than merely a daring solo pilot who made people look to the clouds. "He is no longer permitted to be himself," commented *The New Republic.* "He is US personified. He is the United States."

"Captain Lindbergh personifies the daring of youth," declared Theodore Roosevelt, Jr., Teddy's son and namesake, to reporters at his home in Oyster Bay. "Daniel Boone, David Crockett, and men of that type played a lone hand and made America. Lindbergh is their lineal descendant."

A writer for *Outlook* magazine agreed. "Charles Lindbergh is the heir of all that we like to think is best in America. He is of the stuff out of which have been made the pioneers that opened up the wilderness, first on the Atlantic coast, and then in our great West. His are the qualities which we, as a people, must nourish."

But what is evident to those who look up today at the tiny *Spirit of St. Louis* in Washington's vast Air and Space Museum is how personal was this one American's feat. As he flew alone across the Atlantic, needing to use a periscope because his front view was blocked entirely by added fuel tanks, there was something mystical about his ordeal and his achievement. He had torn pages from his notebook to lighten the load, had trimmed the margins from his maps to save more weight.

In shot, he was playing for keeps.

("I don't think I got any more sleep than Lindbergh," recalled James Stewart who three decades later played him in the movies. "Lindbergh's problem was staying awake; mine was staying asleep that Friday night while he was unreported over the Atlantic between Newfoundland and Ireland." This is simply one of those fascinating juxtapositions—the hero and the actor who would play him. But was there an American who was not rooting for the daring young Lindbergh that night?)

Of course Lindbergh had to navigate the tiny plane as well as fly it. With the chart sitting on his lap he had to make forty adjustments to keep on course from New York to Paris. After eleven hours in the air—only a third of the time he would take to reach Paris—Lindbergh began to feel tired.

Because of the weather he had been forced to postpone the flight the day before. He had stayed awake the entire night. Thirty-six hours without sleep, and now he was riding into nightfall over the lonely Atlantic. If he were to doze off, he would die, given his constant need to control the rudder with his feet.

Three hours later, Lindbergh was flying at ten thousand feet when he realized that sleet was covering his wings. He could feel it pelt on his hand when he reached outside the cockpit. Storm clouds hung above him but it was impossible to judge if he could go around them. He had no radio connection with anyone else on earth to help him figure it out.

"To plunge into these mountains would be like stepping

into quicksand. They enmesh intruders. They're barbaric in their methods. They toss you in their inner turbulence, lash you with their hailstones, poison you with freezing mist. It would be a slow death, a death one would have long minutes to struggle against, trying blindly to regain control of an ice-crippled airplane, climbing, stalling, diving, whipping, always downwards towards the sea."

Then the moon rose. He could now clearly make out the dark hazards ahead. For Lindbergh it was the most moving moment of the flight, a kind of divine blessing on his effort. He no longer had to wonder whether he was awake or asleep, alive or dead.

In Paris—a city he identified from the air by spotting the Eiffel Tower—he was met by a cheering mob of supporters who exuberantly carried him off the landing field. Around the world, people devoured news accounts of his daring flight. Lindbergh had made history, and he had done it alone.

"To millions of simple people he was no longer flying for himself but for humanity," wrote his biographer Leonard Mosley, "he was not simply flying to Paris but blazing the trail to a better life."

Amelia Earhart

On May 20, 1932, exactly five years after the date of Lindbergh's historic New York-to-Paris flight, Amelia Earhart set

out for Paris from Newfoundland. Because of the wind and ice, she wound up setting down in an Irish cow pasture.

"Where am I?" she asked a surprised local man as she climbed out of her plane. "In Gallagher's pasture," he answered. "Have you come far?"

Earhart, the first woman to receive the Distinguished Flying Cross from Congress, embodied the American trailblazing spirit. Once, accepting an honor, she described how a French newspaper had speculated on whether she could bake a cake. "So I accept these awards on behalf of the cake bakers and all of those other women who can do some things quite as important, if not more important, than flying, as well as in the name of women flying today."

Though she enrolled as a medical student at Columbia University's College of Physicians and Surgeons, Earhart found herself unable to shake the belief that she'd been born to the cockpit and not the operating theater. "Aviation had come close to me" is how she describes the effects of meeting a group of dashing young military pilots when she was a nurse's aide during the First World War.

She'd seen an airplane for the first time when she was ten, visiting the Iowa State Fair with her parents. But the urge to fly on her own seized her a decade later, and she soon began to frequent the dusty airfields of the era, where pilot's licenses were as yet unheard of. The guts to go up was all it took.

In 1928, A.E., as she was known, won her earliest international renown when she was recruited to be the token woman
aboard a three-person transatlantic flight. Quickly christened
"Lady Lindy" by adoring headline writers, she was aware that
she hadn't really earned the comparison—at least, not yet.

Her nearly fifteen-hour flight in 1932, when she became
the first woman to fly the Atlantic alone, was beset by technical difficulties, a gas leak among them. It was a true test of
skills aloft.

Her spirit and good humor kept pace with her courage.
"I'm from America," she told the Irish country folk who
were the first to see her after she'd landed in Gallagher's
field.

Here is Earhart soloing above the Pacific three years later,
in 1935:

At no time during the flight did the outside temperature register
below forty degrees Fahrenheit. However, I had the cockpit window open a bit and the cold rain beat in on me until I became
thoroughly chilled. I thought it would be pleasant to have a cup
of hot chocolate. So I did and it was. Indeed that was the most
interesting cup of chocolate I have ever had, sitting up 8,000 feet
over the middle of the Pacific Ocean, quite alone.

In 1937, Earhart, who had both set and broken records
with dashing flair and courage, determined to circle the

globe. "*Why* are you attempting this around the world flight?" she asked herself, her posthumously published autobiography tells us. "Because I want to. Here was shining adventure, beckoning with new experiences, added knowledge of flying, of peoples, of myself."

Somewhere in the vast stretches of the South Pacific, hopping from one island to the next, Earhart's plane disappeared. What survived is indelible, however—the romance of her achievements.

In the nearly seven decades since her disappearance Amelia Earhart has haunted the American imagination.

The Space Race

"An eerie, intermittent croak—it sounded like a cricket with a cold—was picked up by radio receivers around the world last week," *Life* magazine reported in its October 14, 1957, issue. "It came from beyond the stratosphere and signaled an epochal breakthrough into the new age of space exploration. It was being emitted—to the delight of Communists and chagrin of U.S. military men—by a Soviet device which had been shot from the earth as a manmade moon, the first official satellite in history. The Russians had hurled a 23-inch metal sphere into an orbit around the earth some 560 miles up, and at a speed of 18,000 mph it was completing one circuit every hour and 36 minutes. It weighed 184 pounds, eight times as much as the Vanguard satellite the U.S. was still struggling to launch. Inside it were batteries and a radio transmitter broadcasting on 20 and 40 megacycles."

When the Soviets launched Sputnik, Americans were left stunned and demoralized. *We* were supposed to be the first in space. The country became suddenly uneasy about the grandfatherlike leadership of Dwight Eisenhower.

Perhaps we had been too complacent. It was a thought hard to absorb. An ugly shiver down the spines of Americans long convinced of their country's superiority in the face of the Soviet menace. "Artificial satellites will pave the way for space travel," the Soviet news agency *Tass* condescendingly explained to the humiliated West.

Moscow was for the moment, one would have to admit, justified in its self-assurance. If Communism could beat us in the technology of the future, it could also defeat us ideologically as well. The emerging "third world" might decide to look to the Russians for money and advice as they began coming into their own. And where would that leave us?

Four years later, the Soviets sent the cosmonaut Yuri Gagarin into space. This was almost more than our American ego—so twinned with its pioneer heart—could bear.

The new president, John F. Kennedy, had been reared to reject second place. The Soviets may have been up there first, but America's leader stood ready to overtake them.

> I believe that this nation should commit itself to achieving the goal, before this decade is out, of landing a man on the Moon and returning him safely to the Earth. . . . It is a most important decision that we must make as a nation.
>
> I believe we should go to the Moon. But I think every citizen of this country as well as the Members of the Congress should consider the matter carefully in making their judgment, to which we have given attention over many weeks and months, because it is a heavy burden, and there is no sense in agreeing or desiring that the United States take an affirmative position in outer space, unless we are prepared to do the work and bear the burdens to make it successful. If we are not, we should decide today and this year.

Speaking at Rice University in September of 1962, Kennedy asked "But why, some say, the Moon? Why choose this as our goal? And they may well ask why climb the highest mountain? Why, thirty-five years ago, fly the Atlantic?"

> We choose to go to the Moon. We choose to go to the Moon in this decade and do the other things, not because they are easy, but because they are hard, because that goal will serve to orga-

nize and measure the best of our energies and skills, because that challenge is one that we are willing to accept, one we are unwilling to postpone, and one which we intend to win. Many years ago the great British explorer George Mallory, who was to die on Mount Everest, was asked why did he want to climb it. He said, "Because it is there." Well, space is there, and we're going to climb it, and the Moon and the planets are there, and new hopes for knowledge and peace are there. And, therefore, as we set sail we ask God's blessing on the most hazardous and dangerous and greatest adventure on which man has ever embarked.

In July 1969, a year ahead of Kennedy's schedule, the United States—its pioneer honor on the line—landed men on the moon. As a Peace Corps volunteer in Africa, I listened to the shortwave as one of my fellow Americans descended the stairs of the lunar module. "One small step for man, one giant leap for mankind," he said. I can remember my pride.

However, just as there had been great losses as America pushed westward across the continent, so would there be failures and broken dreams within the U.S. space program. In 1967, the astronauts Virgil "Gus" Grissom, Ed White, and Roger Chaffee died in a fatal fire inside their command module. They were testing the vehicle's equipment in preparation for a launch the following month. In 1971, the moon landing of *Apollo* 13 had to be aborted.

But January 1986 would bring the greatest horror.

Seven astronauts aboard the *Challenger* space shuttle died as the craft exploded hardly a minute from the launch pad. The crew included Christa McAuliffe, a high school teacher who had joined as a way to link the nation's children to the conquest of space.

That afternoon, President Ronald Reagan addressed the nation, capturing in a moment of tragedy the spirit of the American space program. He also summed up a great deal about the country itself:

> For the families of the seven, we cannot bear, as you do, the full impact of this tragedy. But we feel the loss, and we're thinking about you so very much. Your loved ones were daring and brave, and they had that special grace, that special spirit that says, "Give me a challenge and I'll meet it with joy." They had a hunger to explore the universe and discover its truths. They wished to serve, and they did. They served all of us.
>
> We've grown used to wonders in this century. It's hard to dazzle us. But for twenty-five years the United States space program has been doing just that. We've grown used to the idea of space, and perhaps we forget that we've only just begun. We're still pioneers. They, the members of the *Challenger* crew, were pioneers.
>
> And I want to say something to the schoolchildren of America who were watching the live coverage of the shuttle's takeoff.

I know it is hard to understand, but sometimes painful things like this happen. It's all part of the process of exploration and discovery. It's all part of taking a chance and expanding man's horizons. The future doesn't belong to the fainthearted; it belongs to the brave. The *Challenger* crew was pulling us into the future, and we'll continue to follow them.

We will never forget them, nor the last time we saw them, this morning, as they prepared for the journey and waved goodbye and "slipped the surly bonds of earth" to "touch the face of God."

A former star of westerns, President Ronald Reagan had a sure grasp for American sentiment. He understood, perhaps more brilliantly than anyone else, the pride the country takes in its pioneer past. We settled the frontier, championed aviation, and entered the vastness of space. If we were ever to give up being pioneers, we would, in an important way, stop being American.

CHAPTER 9

Optimism

Happy days are here again

The skies above are clear again

FRANKLIN D. ROOSEVELT CAMPAIGN SONG

LYRICS, 1932

The Founding Fathers were certified optimists. When they signed the Declaration of Independence on July 4, 1776, they were literally betting their lives that we would win. Rebellion in those thirteen colonies belonging to England was a hanging offense. Yet they sprang into action, guided by a set of principles that included the unalienable right to the "pursuit of happiness."

It is impossible, from the perspective of the early twenty-first century to imagine the audacity of such a guarantee. On July 3, 1776, we were subjects of a European sovereign. When we awoke on July 5, we were free men and women with the right to set our own course—not just as a country, but as individual souls.

A Capital for a Continent

Picture once more that scene of Washington and L'Enfant on horseback on Jenkin's Hill, gazing before them and seeing not a Maryland swampland but a magnificent capital worthy of the society they envisioned.

On July 12, 1790, Washington made the following entry in his diary: ". . . and about noon had two bills presented to me by the joint committee of Congress. The one, 'An Act for Establishing the Temporary & permanent Seat of the Government of the United States.' "

But the first president would not be satisfied with a city the size of Philadelphia, then the largest in the country and the young nation's temporary capital. He was thinking big, and in the days ahead began to take personal charge of the project.

"Philadelphia stood upon an area of three by two miles," he wrote in May 1791, complaining to those on the planning commission when local landowners tried to limit the new capital's size, "and that, if the metropolis of one state occupied so much ground, what ought that of the United States to occupy?"

Pierre L'Enfant, the architect hired to design the capital at Washington, had dreams that matched Washington's. He wanted a city of broad avenues and a capitol building commanding the city's heights: "No nation perhaps had ever before the opportunity offered them of deliberately deciding on the spot where their Capital city should be fixed. The plan should be drawn on such a scale as to leave room for the aggrandizement & embellishment which the increase of the wealth of the Nation will permit it to pursue at any period how ever remote."

At his first meeting with Washington, L'Enfant called for an impressive carriageway connecting the Capitol to the Executive Mansion "proportioned to the Greatnes which a City the Capitale of a powerful Empire ought to manifest." L'Enfant designed radiating avenues that would serve as grand tributaries. As for the buildings themselves, his patron personally approved the layout. "Whilst the Commissioners were engaged in preparing the Deeds to be signed by the Subscribers this afternoon," Washington wrote in his diary on June 28, 1791, "I went out with Major L'Enfant . . . to take a more perfect view of the ground in order to decide finally on the spots on which to place the public buildings."

Franklin D. Roosevelt

In March of 1933, a man stood on the steps of the United States Capitol—on the very Jenkin's Hill that had become the realized vision of Washington and L'Enfant—and declared to a nation staggering from twenty-five percent unemployment and a stock market shrunk to twenty percent its value that the only thing they had "to fear is fear itself."

Franklin Delano Roosevelt was the greatest president of the twentieth century, the quintessential leader for prevailing against both the Great Depression and World War II. It was this man's indomitable optimism that convinced the country it could prevail against the worst economic and military threats in its history.

On the day of Roosevelt's inauguration, the economic situation of the country was sliding downhill fast. The industrial sectors were suffering vast unemployment. Farmers were struggling with rock-bottom prices for their crops and also reeling from the effects of the "Dust Bowl," a drought that destroyed a hundred million acres of topsoil in the Plains states.

The worst had happened: people had begun to lose faith in their country.

"On the farms, in the large metropolitan areas, in the smaller cities and in the villages, millions of our citizens cherish the hope that their old standards of living and of thought have not gone forever," FDR, then the governor of New York, said at the convention that nominated him to run for president. "Those millions cannot and shall not hope in vain."

He meant it. Franklin Roosevelt would place his extraordinary mind and spirit behind a bold plan to reverse the nation's deteriorating condition. "I pledge you, I pledge myself, to a new deal for the American people. Let us all here assembled constitute ourselves prophets of a new order of competence and of courage."

With his New Deal, FDR told Americans that there was indeed hope around the corner. "Out of every crisis, every tribulation, every disaster," he optimistically declared, "mankind rises with some share of greater knowledge, of higher decency, of purer purpose."

The Great Depression would pass, the country would be stronger for it, but the memory of the hardship would endure.

Roosevelt had both optimism and hardship in his own life. Polio had caused his most serious setback. When it struck him at the age of thirty-nine, the recent candidate for vice president was on his way to the top. The young politician refused to accept the fact that he was paraplegic and exercised fanatically. Every day, he put on his heavy braces and attempted to walk to the end of his own driveway. Yet, despite this determination, he never made it past the halfway mark. It didn't stop him.

This optimism never failed him. And when he stood up, supported only by his leg braces, at the 1924 Democratic Convention to give the "Happy Warrior" nominating speech for New York's Governor Al Smith, he achieved his goal. The public saw a man who had endured a hideous ordeal and had proved himself up to it. Throughout his 1932 campaign and on through his long presidency, Franklin Roosevelt would be a man who had "conquered" polio.

If he could do that, he was without question a guy who could take on the Great Depression, the Japanese empire, and Hitler besides.

FDR knew firsthand what the country needed in the 1930s. Like him, it was yearning to get back on its feet. And thanks to him, it did.

"It is not enough to clothe and feed the body of this Nation, and instruct and inform its mind," he said at his third inaugural, "for there is the spirit. And of the three, the greatest is the spirit. Without the body and the mind, as all men know, the Nation could not live. But if the spirit of America were killed, even though the Nation's body and mind, constricted in an alien world, lived on, the America we know would have perished. That spirit—that faith—speaks to us in our daily lives often unnoticed, because they seem so obvious."

His wartime ally, British Prime Minister Winston Churchill, said that meeting FDR was "like opening your first bottle of champagne."

Ask anyone alive during that extraordinary time if they ever doubted that we would win the great war against Hitler and Tojo, and I wager you'll find no one who did.

Yet our thirty-second president's forward-thinking outlook extended beyond victory on the battlefield. Roosevelt strongly believed in the future of a United Nations that could protect freedom around the world. Before the U.S. entered the war in January of 1941, he declared in his "Four Freedoms" speech that what lay ahead was an end to colonialism and the creation of a new community of free nations. "In the future days which we seek to make secure, we look forward to a world founded upon four essential human freedoms."

Freedom of speech and expression, freedom of worship, freedom from want, and freedom from fear: ensuring them remains our optimistic goal to this day.

Ronald Reagan

"I have always believed that this land was placed here between the two great oceans by some divine plan," Ronald Reagan declared at the end of a 1980 television debate.

It was placed here to be found by a special kind of people—people who had a special love for freedom and who had the courage to uproot themselves and leave hearth and homeland and come

to what in the beginning was the most undeveloped wilderness possible.

We spoke in a multitude of tongues—landed on this eastern shore and then went out over the mountains and prairies and the deserts and the far western mountains of the Pacific, building cities and towns and farms and schools and churches.

If wind, water and fire destroyed them, we built them again. And in so doing at the same time we built a new breed of human called an American—a proud, an independent and a most compassionate individual for the most part. Two hundred years ago Tom Paine, when the thirteen tiny colonies were trying to become a nation, said we have it in our power to begin the world over again. Together we can begin the world over again. We can meet our destiny and that destiny can build a land here that will be for all mankind a shining city on a hill. I think we ought to get at it.

He had personal reasons for that optimism. A kid from the Midwest, son of an alcoholic father, he got himself through college, then became a regional celebrity as a radio sports announcer. More ambitious than that, he went to Hollywood, wangled a screen test, and joined the list of contract movie stars.

When the film roles stopped coming, he moved over to television and became an even bigger national personality as host of *General Electric Theater*. Next came politics, which saw him winning two terms as California governor and, finally, two terms in the White House. He remains, along with John F. Kennedy, the most popular of recent American presidents.

Just a few months into his presidency, Reagan was shot as he was leaving a Washington hotel. One of the bullets lodged within inches of his heart. Had it not been for the courage and quick thinking of the Secret Service who got him to George Washington University Hospital in just over ten minutes, he would not have made it.

Yet one reason the country never realized just how close he had come to dying was Reagan's attitude in those most ghastly of circumstances. "I hope you're a Republican," he kidded the surgeon about to operate. Then, later: "Honey, I forgot to duck," he told his wife Nancy.

"The grace and humor Reagan showed after the attempt to assassinate him in 1981 had, more than any other single event, added a mythical quality to his leadership, revealing his character in a way that made it impossible to dislike him," wrote his biographer Garry Wills.

Reagan also showed amazing grace when he learned he'd been struck by Alzheimer's disease. Knowing that from then on he'd be gradually losing his grasp on everyday life, the former president sat down and wrote a letter to his country:

Nov. 5, 1994

My Fellow Americans,

I have recently been told that I am one of the millions of Americans who will be afflicted with Alzheimer's Disease.

Upon learning this news, Nancy and I had to decide whether as private citizens we would keep this a private matter or whether we would make this news known in a public way.

In the past Nancy suffered from breast cancer and I had my cancer surgeries. We found through our open disclosures we were able to raise public awareness. We were happy that as a result many more people underwent testing.

They were treated in early stages and able to return to normal, healthy lives.

So now, we feel it is important to share it with you. In opening our hearts, we hope this might promote greater awareness of this condition. Perhaps it will encourage a clearer understanding of the individuals and families who are affected by it.

At the moment I feel just fine. I intend to live the remainder of the years God gives me on this earth doing the things I have always done. I will continue to share life's journey with my beloved Nancy and my family. I plan to enjoy the great outdoors and stay in touch with my friends and supporters.

Unfortunately, as Alzheimer's Disease progresses, the family often bears a heavy burden. I only wish there was some way I could spare Nancy from this painful experience. When the time comes I am confident that with your help she will face it with faith and courage.

In closing let me thank you, the American people, for giving me the great honor of allowing me to serve as your President. When the Lord calls me home, whenever that may be, I will leave with the greatest love for this country of ours and eternal optimism for its future.

I now begin the journey that will lead me into the sunset of my life. I know that for America there will always be a bright dawn ahead. Thank you, my friends.

May God always bless you.

Sincerely,

Ronald Reagan

Like George Washington, Reagan understood the value of reputation. An American president needs to act nobly, display a certain selfless disregard. Just as the first president earned his country's honor with his willingness to surrender his power, so Reagan showed his by his willingness to leave the public stage.

President George W. Bush paid tribute to his predecessor when he awarded Ronald Reagan the Medal of Freedom after the September 2001 terrorist attacks on New York and Washington. "He would look at the spirit and sacrifice of the fire-fighters, police officers, men and women of our military, average Americans, and he'd be proud. He wouldn't be surprised. He knew the courage and decency and generosity at the heart of this country because he shared it and he embodied it."

Yanks

Yanks is a British-made movie about American GIs training in England in the months before D-Day. There's a terrific scene that takes place between a young American mess sergeant, played by Richard Gere, and his English girlfriend. She's asking him about his plans after the war, assuming that he'll do what every working-class English lad does, that is, follow in his father's footsteps.

JEAN: After the war, are you going back to work for your dad?

MATT: Not a chance. I haven't told anybody this before. You know what a *motel* is, kind of like a hotel on the highway. You know, stop off and you, you got your own little cabin and bathroom. Springin' up all over the states, and I'm gonna build me one of them. I got a place all picked out too. Canyon, the top of a canyon kinda flattens out. I'm gonna build right there. It's beautiful. . . . When that one gets goin', I'm gonna build another one, and another one, and another one . . .

The English girl is taken aback by the young American's speech. No one has ever spoken to her with such optimism, such disregard of possible obstacles, such pure confidence.

"I'm sure you will," she tells him.

In the spring of 1945, with the war in its last months, Franklin Roosevelt received the seventeen-year-old son of his Secretary of the Navy James V. Forrestal in the Oval Office. The boy was about to ship out. An Arctic convoy was awaiting him. Like most young Americans he had no real knowledge of FDR's physical condition, which had deteriorated considerably by that time. He began to mumble something to his host about the war.

"Don't talk to me about the war," FDR exploded with delight, "Tell me what you're going to do after we've won!"

CHAPTER 10

American Exceptionalism

Let us reject the blinders of isolationism, just as we have refused the crown of an empire. Let us not dominate others with our power or betray them with our indifference. And let us have an American foreign policy that reflects American character. The modesty of true strength. The humility of *real greatness*.

PRESIDENTIAL CANDIDATE GEORGE W. BUSH,
NOVEMBER 19, 1999, AT THE RONALD REAGAN
PRESIDENTIAL LIBRARY

We are both reluctant warriors and people of action. We lionize heroic loners and champion the underdog. We are lured by the undiscovered, exalt the potential of the average American, and cherish the right to be who or what we dream of being. Through it all, we remain the most optimistic people on the planet.

As you have seen, the iconic figures in this book—from Washington to Jack Kennedy—exemplify a number of these notions. The reason is obvious. One classic American notion—a rebellious spirit, for example—feeds naturally into another—rooting for the underdog—and into another still—

an optimistic heart. The desire to avoid foreign entanglements fits with the desire to avoid entangling government
here at home.

It's the combination of all the notions, plus one we haven't
mentioned, that gives us what might be called an American
character. This missing notion, often referred to as American
exceptionalism, is that this country may have come into
being by God or history for a special purpose.

From our beginnings, Americans have counted this country special, even blessed. In the early seventeenth century,
Puritans arriving in Massachusetts agreed that their coming
to the New World charged them with a spiritual and political
destiny. They were to build a society that would be the model
for the world.

It was while still at sea on the *Arabella* that John Winthrop
gave his famous sermon. In it, he said:

Now the only way to avoid this shipwreck and to provide for our
posterity is to follow the counsel of Micah, to do Justly, to love
mercy, to walk humbly with our God. . . . That we shall be as a
City upon a Hill, the eyes of all people are upon us; so that if we
shall deal falsely with our God in this work we have undertaken
and so cause him to withdraw his present help from us, we shall
be made a story and a byword through the world, we shall open
the mouths of enemies to speak evil of the ways of God and all
professors for God's sake . . .

Nearly four centuries later, this notion of America as an exceptional country carries potent force. The notion that this country was founded as much more than merely a place to dwell and prosper drives our dealings with other countries, elevating both our morality and our morale here at home. It is a spring that has fed our history, including the American Revolution and its assertion of individual liberty, the abolitionists' condemnation of slavery, and the civil rights movement of the 1960s.

The Power to Begin the World Over Again

By 1776, the notion of an American mission, as invoked by Winthrop, had come to sound a more secular note. In January of that year Thomas Paine published *Common Sense*. As we have seen, this widely circulated pamphlet called for a revolution not just against England but against the tide of human history. The new American republic would be independent of Europe but also of the past. "We have every opportunity and every encouragement before us to form the noblest purest constitution on the face of the earth," Paine wrote, "We have it in our power to begin the world over again."

That meant designing a new type of government, wholly distinct from the European monarchies. It would include the "self-evident" truth that "all men are created equal, that they are endowed by their Creator with certain unalienable Rights, that among these are Life, Liberty and the pursuit of Happiness."

In all the world, in all of history, this would be the exceptional country that upheld those God-given rights.

America is "the only nation in the world that is founded on a creed," G.K. Chesterton wrote a century and a half later. "That creed is set forth with dogmatic and even theological lucidity in the Declaration of Independence."

That a country could be founded on a commitment to rights never before recognized, that it would offer itself as a model for self-government, is a grand notion indeed. Yet American history could not have begun without it.

Benjamin Franklin and
Secular Exceptionalism

While Winthrop and Jefferson based their notion of American exceptionalism to differing degrees on theology, Ben Franklin saw a secular mission for the country. "I never doubted . . . the existence of the Deity, that he made the world and governed it by his Providence; (but) the most acceptable service of God was the doing good to *man*."

To Franklin the mission of America was to be a country where a person could fully become who he or she wished to be. According to scholar Deborah Madsen, Franklin's *Auto-*

biography "represents Franklin's life as enacting the newly formed American myth of individual self-realization in a land of opportunity. It is the secular America that will be a model of democratic government and the envy of all the nations of the earth." Franklin's account of his personal rise from "poverty and obscurity" to wealth and international fame has long been seen as an American primer.

To the great Franklin, the unique promise of American life was that an Archie Leach might become a Cary Grant. Or that Harry Truman, a haberdasher from a little town in Missouri, could one day become president, with the fate of the world in his hands.

For Ben Franklin—and for me also—America is and should be a shining beacon that attracts newcomers from all over the world. But Franklin also wisely understood that the American way of life would not be easy.

In "Information on Those Who Would Remove to America," which he wrote in 1784, Franklin warned potential immigrants that they would not be accorded any special regard or position because of some inherited European rank or title. He advised that, instead, they cultivate virtues like thriftiness and common sense.

A century later Robert Ingersoll, an agnostic, would look back on the historic coincidences that drove the new country into existence.

AMERICAN

There were the Puritans who hated the Episcopalians, and Episcopalians who hated the Catholics; and the Catholics who hated both, while the Quakers held them all in contempt.

There they were, of every sort, and color and kind, and how was it that they came together? They had a common aspiration. They wanted to form a new nation. More than that, most of them cordially hated Great Britain; and they pledged each other to forget these religious prejudices, for a time at least, and agreed that there should be only one religion until they got through; and that was the religion of patriotism.

Abolitionism

The notion of America's historic destiny was the driving argument against slavery. How could a country blessed with an exceptional mission as role model, guarantor of rights and opportunity, defend such an evil institution? The belief that America was driven by a national ideal, whether religious or secular, drove the early-nineteenth-century movement to end slavery.

Abolitionism carried with it not just a moral but also a national appeal to Americans, a call to bring their society into conformity with its grandest notion of itself.

We hear that appeal in the words of Frederick Douglass:

> We wonder how such saints can sing,
> Or praise the Lord upon the wing,

Who roar, and scold, and whip, and sting,
And to their slaves and mammon cling,
In guilty conscience union.

Even in the turmoil of civil war, Abraham Lincoln reminded the people of their country's exceptional mission. In his Second Annual Message to Congress he spoke of the Union as "the last, best hope of earth." In his great Second Inaugural he questioned how any American could be asked to defend slavery. "It may seem strange that any man should dare to ask a just God's assistance in wringing their bread from the sweat of other men's faces."

With the "peculiar" institution of slavery dispatched at the cost of six hundred thousand American lives, the country was now itself free, free to embrace its notion of itself as an exceptional country.

In the 1960s, the movement for civil rights in the South took on the same grand purpose. Once again, how could this country—feeling itself inspired by God, or the very best in man—defend Jim Crow laws that so debased such a large segment of the American people? That was the point President Kennedy raised in his June 1963 televised address to the nation. He called civil rights "a moral issue . . . as old as the Scriptures and . . . as clear as the American Constitution."

Kennedy asked how a country could defend its reputation as a beacon of individual liberty when it allowed so many of its own people to be robbed of it. "Today we are committed to a worldwide struggle to promote and protect the rights of all who wish to be free. And when Americans are sent to Vietnam or West Berlin, we do not ask for whites only. We preach freedom around the world, and we mean it."

Two months later, Martin Luther King appealed from the steps of the Lincoln Memorial—the closest we have to a national shrine—for America to come alive to the ideals on which our great nation was founded.

This will be the day when all of God's children will be able to sing with a new meaning, "My country, 'tis of thee, sweet land of liberty, of thee I sing. Land where my fathers died, land of the pilgrim's pride, from every mountainside, let freedom ring."

And if America is to be a great nation this must become true. So let freedom ring from the prodigious hilltops of New Hampshire. Let freedom ring from the mighty mountains of New York. Let freedom ring from the heightening Alleghenies of Pennsylvania! Let freedom ring from the snowcapped Rockies of Colorado! Let freedom ring from the curvaceous peaks of California!

But not only that; let freedom ring from Stone Mountain of Georgia! Let freedom ring from Lookout Mountain of Tennessee!

Let freedom ring from every hill and every molehill of Mississippi. From every mountainside, let freedom ring.

When we let freedom ring, when we let it ring from every village and every hamlet, from every state and every city, we will be able to speed up that day when all of God's children, black men and white men, Jews and Gentiles, Protestants and Catholics, will be able to join hands and sing in the words of the old Negro spiritual, "Free at last! Free at last! Thank God Almighty, we are free at last!"

With the new century, I believe, America is confronted by new concerns arising from its own *exceptionalist* notion. Even as we defend ourselves against terrorist infiltration, we must guard those individual rights that stand at the heart of our national mission. Even as we pursue those who had a hand in the attacks of September 11, 2001, we must guard our history as a country who fights only to defend itself.

America also suffers from a pair of self-inflicted problems. Look around—we use an outrageous share of the world's fossil fuel on our highways. We have also permitted a revolting greed to invade the highest corporate offices. It was as if, starting in the 1990s, families pegged their status to the size and fuel-*in*efficiency of their SUVs. At the same time, too many CEOs had pegged their status to "compensation" packages inconceivable to most Americans.

Such behavior is neither exemplary nor sustainable. One leads to massive foreign oil dependence and the wars needed to protect it. The other stirs the sort of Jacksonian rebellion we saw in the 1820s. The average person will respect capitalism only as long as capitalism respects *him.*

That said, I believe that America exceeds the great notions it set for itself two centuries and a quarter ago. American democracy and human rights benefit from the best "word of mouth" in the world.

Though we are often criticized for seeing the world in black and white, it is the United States that still gets called upon to rid the world of its Hitlers, Stalins, Milosevices, and bin Ladens. Despite all the hostility of the Islamic world over our support of Israel and the oil potentates of the Persian Gulf, we remain the one country where most people want to study and to live. We are still the place where a person can arrive, learn English, change their name if they wish, and confect the work, identity, and lifestyle they choose.

Every national or ethnic group that comes to America enjoys immensely greater prosperity here than it did in the old country. That includes all the immigrants from Europe, Asia, the Mideast, and the Americas.

The best sense of our national purpose can be found in the hearts of most Americans. When the attacks of September 11 came, the country united. We returned in spirit to the notions of our youth. We cheered the firefighters, were made proud by the go-for-broke passengers of Flight 93.

When many of us men were five years old, we wanted to be firemen when we grew up. We wanted to be brave for people. Girls that age wanted to be nurses for the same reason. A Gallup poll taken in December 2001, after September 11, asked people which professions held the highest moral prestige. The results were Number 1, Firefighter; Number 2, Nurse.

When the corporate scandals broke in the spring and summer of 2002, Americans were disgusted and outraged. They wanted those traitors to free enterprise put in jail where they belonged.

This is the good news: we are still Americans.

The same spirit that built this great country continues to rip across it today, the same destiny lures us, and the same optimistic, rebellious nature drives us that did even in those early, scary days when our country's body was small but its soul was large.

So this is why we're different.

We're rebels, loners, reluctant warriors, pioneers, and optimists. We believe in the man—or woman—of action, trust in the merit of the common individual, root for the underdog. We are a self-made people who see our country assigned to some great mission.

I found a joy in discovering these grand American notions, a confidence in not discovering them alone. Venturing back into America's past, I realized I was tagging along with a rather impressive posse. For two centuries we have constructed our national character on the raw material of our country's roots.

James Fenimore Cooper's Hawkeye owed his exploits to Daniel Boone, his rustic's pride to the age of Andrew Jackson.

F. Scott Fitzgerald's Jay Gatsby was not the first American to believe in the second chance. Thomas Paine saw the country itself as an opportunity to "begin the world all over."

Frank Capra's Jefferson Smith was but honoring the call of

his great Virginia namesake for "a little rebellion now and then."

President Kennedy's gutsy drive to the moon was a conspicuous salute to the spirit of "The Lone Eagle," Charles Lindbergh.

Senator John McCain's brazen 2002 assault on "crony capitalism" is tribute to that earlier Republican reformer Teddy Roosevelt.

Colin Powell's description of war is precisely what George Washington once said. Both generals called it a "last resort."

We are a people raised on such grand American notions. They comprise the most vital, most provocative, most consequential self-portrait in human history.

Bringing that self-portrait to life in these pages has been a grand experience. Other writers might have chosen different movies, different books, different snatches of history. What you've read here reflects my upbringing, my tastes, my sentiments.

I don't claim to be impartial about my country. I confess to being in cahoots with my subject from the beginning.

Remember that smile of Jay Gatsby's? How he looked at Nick Carraway with an irresistible prejudice in his favor, how he saw him just as Nick himself hoped to be seen at his best?

In these pages, I hope I have cast just such a smile at my country.

NOTES

Prologue

1   "France was a land": F. Scott Fitzgerald, "The Swimmers," *Saturday Evening Post,* October 19, 1929.

2   All *Casablanca* synopsis and dialogue: *Casablanca.* Director Michael Curtiz. Performers Humphrey Bogart, Ingrid Bergman, and Paul Henreid. Warner Bros., 1942.

3   "permanent alliances": George Washington, Washington's Farewell Address, Sept. 17, 1796, from the George Washington Papers at the Library of Congress, 1741–1799.

3   "I want an American character that the powers of Europe may be convinced": George Washington, letter to Patrick Henry, October 9, 1795, from the George Washington Papers at the Library of Congress, 1741–1799.

3   "War should be the politics of last resort": Colin Powell, *My American Journey* (New York: Random House, 1995), quoted in *The Washington Post,* October 7, 2001.

3   All *Mr. Smith Goes to Washington* synopsis and dialogue: *Mr. Smith Goes to Washington.* Director Frank Capra. Performers Jean Arthur, James Stewart, and Claude Rains. Columbia, 1939.

3   rot at the top: Robert Reich, *Tales of a New America* (New York: Times Books, 1987), pp. 11–12.

4   "a little rebellion now and then": Thomas Jefferson, letter to James Madison, January 30, 1787, from Julian P. Boyd, ed. *Papers of Thomas Jefferson, Volume 11* (Princeton, N.J.: Princeton University Press, 1955), p. 93.

6   "This great nation will endure as it has endured": Franklin Delano Roosevelt, First Inaugural Address, March 4, 1933.

6   "a city upon a hill": John Winthrop, "Modell of Christian Charity," sermon for the Massachusetts Bay Colony, 1630.

Chapter 1. A Self-Made Country

11   "The truth was that Jay Gatsby of West Egg, Long Island": *Gatsby*, p. 104.

12   "Do you know what's wrong with you?": Graham McCann, *Cary Grant: A Class Apart* (New York: Columbia University Press, 1996), p. 3.

12   "Cary's the only thing": McCann, pp. 3–4.

13   "I pretended to be somebody I wanted to be": Cary Grant, *The New York Times,* December 1, 1986.

13   "I cultivated raising one eyebrow": McCann, pp. 62–63.

14   "Listen!": *His Girl Friday* dialogue, from McCann, p. 65.

14   "It was a knowing wink to the audience": McCann, p. 65.

14   "I don't know how I consider death": Cary Grant, *The Washington Post,* December 1, 1986.

14   "Everybody wants to be Cary Grant": McCann, p. 4.

15   "pedestal waiting for a monument": Pierre L'Enfant in his report to George Washington, June 22, 1791, from Hans Paul Caemmerer, *The Life of Pierre Charles L'Enfant* (New York: Da Capo Press, 1950), p. 152.

16   "monumental concept": Bob Ellis, "Washington: Who Cares About Their Capital?," *Bonjour Paris,* January 1999.

16   "begin the world over again": Thomas Paine, *Rights of Man, Common Sense, and Other Political Writings* (Oxford: Oxford University Press, 1995), p. 53.

18   "I would have accepted without question": F. Scott Fitzgerald, *The Great Gatsby* (New York: Simon & Schuster, 1995), p. 54.

18   "I'll tell you God's truth": *Gatsby,* p. 69.

18   "I wouldn't ask too much of her": *Gatsby,* p. 116.

18   "I'm going to fix everything": *Gatsby,* p. 117.

19   "It was one of those rare smiles": *Gatsby,* p. 52.

19   "Gatsby was not a character": Alfred Kazin, "Hemingway, Fitzgerald: The Cost of Being American," *American Heritage* 35, Apr./May 1984, p. 64.

20   "heightened sensitivity": *Gatsby,* p. 6.

22   "You have got to get rid of that terrible *twang*!": Robert Lacey, *Grace* (Thorndike, Me.: G.K. Hall, 1995), p. 62.

22   "It takes a trained ear": Lacey, p. 62.

23   "When Grace Kelly pronounced the word 'rotten' ": Lacey, pp. 62–63.

23   "Gracie's new voice": Lacey, p. 63.

23   "British accent": Lacey, p. 63.

23   "I must talk this way for my work": Lacey, p. 63.

23   "She got away from home early": John B. "Jack" Kelly, from Lacey, p. 56.

25   "My look is not really European": Ralph Lauren, quoted in Freedman.

26   Americans will "pay to transform": Neal Gabler, "Molding Our

Lives in the Image of Movies," *The New York Times,* October 25, 1998.

26 "cunningly cinematic": Elizabeth Grice, *The Daily Telegraph* (London), May 6, 1999, p. 25.

Chapter 2. The Constant Rebel

31 "I hold it that a little rebellion": Thomas Jefferson, letter to James Madison, January 30, 1787, from Julian P. Boyd, ed. *Papers of Thomas Jefferson, Volume 11* (Princeton, N.J.: Princeton University Press, 1955), p. 93.

31 All *Mr. Smith Goes to Washington* synopsis and dialogue: *Mr. Smith Goes to Washington.* Director Frank Capra, Performers Jean Arthur, James Stewart, and Claude Rains. Columbia, 1939.

34 "Dear Mr. Cohn": Joseph P. Kennedy, cable to Harry Cohn, from Frank Capra, *The Name Above the Title: An Autobiography* (New York: Macmillan, 1971), p. 292.

35 The critics: *Kansas City Journal, Variety,* Hedda Hopper of Esquire Features, Inc., *Cincinnati Post, Los Angeles Times,* from Capra, pp. 279, 290.

39 "Government even in its best state": Thomas Paine, *Common Sense* (Philadelphia: Printed, and Sold, by R. Bell, 1776).

39 "Man did not enter into society": Thomas Paine, *The Rights of Man, being an answer to Mr. Burke's attack on the French Revolution* (Dublin: [s.n.], 1791).

40 "Unsuccessful rebellions, indeed, generally establish the encroachments": Thomas Jefferson, letter to James Madison, January 30, 1787, from Julian P. Boyd, ed. *Papers of Thomas*

Jefferson, Volume 11 (Princeton, N.J.: Princeton University Press, 1955), p. 93.

42 "triumphantly established Jackson": Arthur M. Schlesinger, Jr., *The Age of Jackson* (Boston: Little, Brown and Company, 1945), p. 115.

42 "Jackson was widely acclaimed": Joseph J. Tregle, Jr., biography of Andrew Jackson, *Grolier's/Encyclopedia Americana*, available online.

43 The platform: People's Party Platform of 1896, adopted at St. Louis, Mo., July 24, 1896.

43 "Cross of Gold" Speech: William Jennings Bryan, Democratic National Convention, Chicago, Ill., July 9, 1896.

45 "I'm a small fish here in Washington": Huey Long, from "Huey Long: Every Man a King," the Social Security Administration website, available online.

45 "Every Man a King": Original phrase from Bryan's 1900 Democratic presidential nomination address. "Behold a Republic: Whose every man is a king, but no one wears a crown!"

45 "How many men ever went to a barbecue": Huey Long, speech to Senate staffers, Washington, D.C., December 11, 1934.

46 "rot at the top": Robert Reich, *Tales of a New America* (New York: Times Books, 1987), pp. 11–12.

46 "The struggle is only occasionally and incidentally": Reich, pp. 11–12.

48 "I knew that every prisoner": John McCain with Mark Salter, *Faith of My Fathers* (New York: Random House, 1999), p. 235.

49 "It was hard to take": McCain, p. 254.

50 "In prison, I fell in love": McCain, p. 254.

50   "I still shared the ideals of America": McCain, p. 255.

51   "Trust was sacrificed": McCain, quoted in *The New York Times,*
     July 12, 2002.

53   "Storms of spontaneous applause": *The Hollywood Reporter,*
     November 4, 1942, from Capra, p. 292.

Chapter 3. The Reluctant Warrior

57   All *Casablanca* synopsis and dialogue: *Casablanca,* Director
     Michael Curtiz. Performers Humphrey Bogart, Ingrid Bergman,
     and Paul Henreid. Warner Bros., 1942.

60   "Let's roll!": Todd Beamer, onboard United Airlines Flight 93,
     September 11, 2001, The Associated Press, September 20, 2001.

60   "This nation is peaceful, but fierce when stirred to anger":
     George W. Bush, memorial service at Washington National
     Cathedral, September 14, 2001.

61   "We can't hear you . . . I can hear *you!": Unknown crowd mem-
     ber and George W. Bush, at Ground Zero, September 14, 2001,
     The New York Times, September 15, 2001.

61   It was first flown in December 1775: Stanley Godbold, Jr. and
     Robert H. Woody, *Christopher Gadsden and the American Rev-
     olution* (Knoxville, Tenn.: University of Tennessee Press, 1982),
     p. 142.

62   Benjamin Franklin's letter: "The Rattle-Snake as a Symbol of
     America," *Pennsylvania Journal,* December 27, 1775.

63   "If he does that, he will be the greatest man in the world":
     King George III, from Garry Wills, *Cincinnatus George Wash-
     ington and the Enlightenment* (New York: Doubleday, 1984),
     p. 13.

64 Washington's Farewell Address, September 17, 1796: from the George Washington Papers at the Library of Congress, 1741–1799.

64 "I shall constantly bear in mind": George Washington, letter to Continental Congress Governing Committee, January 1, 1777, from the George Washington Papers at the Library of Congress, 1741–1799.

65 "permanent alliances": George Washington, Washington's Farewell Address, September 17, 1796, from the George Washington Papers at the Library of Congress, 1741–1799.

65 "In a word, I want an *American* character": George Washington, letter to Patrick Henry, October 9, 1795, from the George Washington Papers at the Library of Congress, 1741–1799.

65 "No one better taught than Washington": Wills, p. 226.

65 "When we assumed the Soldier, we did not lay aside the Citizen": George Washington, letter to New York Provincial Congress, June 26, 1775, from the George Washington Papers at the Library of Congress, 1741–1799.

66 "Peace, commerce and honest friendship with all nations": Thomas Jefferson, First Inaugural Address, March 4, 1801, from the Thomas Jefferson Papers Series 1, General Correspondence at the Library of Congress, 1651–1827.

67 make the world "safe for democracy": Woodrow Wilson, official biography from the White House, available online.

67 "not nostrums, but normalcy": Warren G. Harding, campaign speech in Boston, May 14, 1920.

68 "I want to suggest that there is in America a *dream of freedom*": Michael Wood, *America in the Movies* (New York: Basic Books, 1975), p. 28.

69   "It might not have acquired its cult status": Henry Allen, *The Washington Post,* April 12, 1992.

71   Weinberger's and Powell's new criteria for overseas military involvement: developed in part from a speech Caspar Weinberger gave at the National Press Club, November 28, 1984, *The New York Times,* November 29, 1984.

72   "War should be the politics of last resort": Colin Powell, *My American Journey* (New York: Random House, 1995), quoted in *The Washington Post,* October 7, 2001.

72   "When the political objective is important": Colin Powell, "U.S. Forces: Challenges Ahead; Enormous Power, Sobering Responsibility," *Foreign Affairs,* Winter 1992, p. 32.

75   "to use all necessary and appropriate force": Senate and the House of Representatives of the United States of America in Congress, assembled, S.J.Res.23, Short Title: "Authorization for Use of Military Force," September 14, 2001.

75   "We will direct every resource": George W. Bush, Address to a Joint Session of Congress and the American People, September 20, 2001.

76   "axis of evil", etc.: George W. Bush, State of the Union Address, January 29, 2002.

76   Just a few weeks later a high State Department official appended: Undersecretary of State John R. Bolton, in a speech to the Heritage Foundation, *Detroit Free Press,* May 7, 2002.

76   "tyrants", "human liberty", etc.: George W. Bush, Remarks at 2002 Graduation Exercise of the United States Military Academy, West Point, June 1, 2002.

Chapter 4. Action

81 "Shift that fat ass, Harry": George Washington, from A. J. Langguth, *Patriots: The Men Who Started the American Revolution* (New York: Simon & Schuster, 1988), p. 411.

82 *Wrestling Ernest Hemingway*. Director Randa Haines. Performers Robert Duvall, Richard Harris, and Shirley MacLaine. Warner Brothers, 1993.

82 "I desire to do pioneering or exploring work": Ernest Hemingway, from Megan Floyed Desnoyers, *Ernest Hemingway: A Storyteller's Legacy*, the John F. Kennedy Library, available online.

83 "I can't get away from the fact that you're just a boy": Agnes von Kurowsky, from Jamie Allen, "Hemingway Biography: From Illinois to International Celebrity," *A Hemingway Retrospective*, CNN online.

83 "Then there was a flash, as when a blast-furnace door is swung open": Ernest Hemingway from Alfred Kazin, "Hemingway and Fitzgerald: The Cost of Being American," *American Heritage* 35, April/May 1984, p. 51.

84 "If he hadn't been in Paris when he was": Michael Reynolds, from Allen.

84 "I was trying to write then and I found the greatest difficulty": Ernest Hemingway, *Death in the Afternoon* (New York: Scribner, 1932), p. 2.

85 "drank like his heroes and heroines": Malcolm Cowley, from Jeffrey Meyers, "Memoirs of Hemingway: The Growth of a Legend," *The Virginia Quarterly Review* 60:4 (Charlottesville, Va.: University of Virginia, 1984), pp. 588–89.

86 "the best I can write ever for all of my life": Hemingway to Wallace Meyer, March 4 and 7, 1952, Outgoing Correspondence, Hemingway Collection, John F. Kennedy Library, cited in Desnoyers.

86 "Let any of you decide for yourselves": Norman Mailer, *Advertisements for Myself* (Cambridge, Mass.: Harvard University Press, 1992), p. 21.

86 "Ernest Hemingway became and remains": Michael Reynolds, "Hemingway in Our Times," *The New York Times,* July 11, 1999.

88 "I went out onto the sidewalk": Ernest Hemingway, *The Sun Also Rises* (New York: Charles Scribner's Sons, 1926), pp. 29–30.

91 "Lord Cornwallis once observed after Yorktown": Winston Churchill, from James C. Hume, *Churchill* (New York: Stein and Day Publishers, 1980), p. 267.

92 6 foot three inches and weighing 280 pounds: Langguth, p. 410.

93 They were to kill any rebel they got their hands on: Langguth, pp. 425–6.

93 "We've got the old fox safe now": General Charles Cornwallis, from Langguth, p. 426.

94 two thousand dead and injured . . . lost only six with 10 wounded: Joseph J. Tregle, Jr., biography of Andrew Jackson, *Grolier's/Encyclopedia Americana,* available online.

96 "No terms except an unconditional and immediate surrender": Ulysses S. Grant, from David Donald, biography of Ulysses S. Grant, *Grolier's/Encyclopedia Americana,* available online.

96 "I can't spare this man": Abraham Lincoln, from Donald.

97 "Mr. Roosevelt is the Tom Sawyer of the political world": Mark

Twain, from Bruce Miroff, "Theodore Roosevelt, Heroic Leadership and Masculine Spectacle," *Icons of Democracy: American Leaders as Heroes, Aristocrats, Dissenters, and Democrats* (New York: Basic Books, 1993), p. 159.

97   "It is not the critic who counts": Theodore Roosevelt, from Miroff, p. 161.

99   "easy contempt?": Theodore Roosevelt, from Edmund Morris, *The Rise of Theodore Roosevelt* (New York: Ballantine Books, 1979), p. 63.

99   "the fellowship of the doers": from Morris, p. 63.

99   "Finnegan hesitated for a second": Theodore Roosevelt, *Century* magazine, from Miroff, p. 169.

99   They included cowboys from his Dakota days, a quartet of policemen: Miroff, p. 170.

100   "a permanent historical work": Miroff, p. 169.

100   "Shout hurrah for Erin Go Bragh!": Theodore Roosevelt, from Morris, p. 616.

100   "To the officers—may they get killed, wounded or promoted": Theodore Roosevelt, from Morris, p. 616.

100   "that damned cowboy": Theodore Roosevelt, quoted in William H. Harbaugh, biography of Theodore Roosevelt, *Grolier's/Encyclopedia Americana,* available online.

102   "I do not care a rap about being shot": Theodore Roosevelt, from Miroff, p. 166.

102   It was Senator Henry Cabot Lodge: account of Lodge's masterful engineering of the Eisenhower presidential campaign from Herbert Parmet, *Eisenhower and the American Crusade* (New York: Macmillan, 1972), pp. 46–56.

103 "get this country moving again": John F. Kennedy, fourth televised 1960 presidential debate, transcript from the John F. Kennedy Library, available online.

104 It was John Hersey's: "A Reporter At Large," *The New Yorker* magazine, June 17, 1944, pp. 31–43.

104 "World War II was their greatest campaign manager": Sutton, from Christopher J. Matthews, *Kennedy & Nixon: The Rivalry That Shaped Postwar America* (New York: Simon & Schuster, 1996), pp. 31–32.

105 "I firmly believe that as much as I was shaped by anything": John F. Kennedy, letter to Lady Nancy Astor, September 12, 1954 as quoted in Edward J. Renehan, Jr., *The Kennedys at War: 1937–1945* (New York: Doubleday, 2002), p. 2.

Chapter 5. The Common Man

109 "For the first six months": Majority Whip J. Hamilton "Ham" Lewis to Harry Truman, from David McCullough, *Truman* (New York: Simon & Schuster, 1992), p. 214.

109 All *Dave* synopsis and dialogue: *Dave.* Director Ivan Reitman. Performers Kevin Kline, Sigourney Weaver, Ben Kingsley, and Frank Langella. Warner Bros., 1993.

112 There were only thirty-eight in all: from A. J. Langguth, *Patriots: The Men Who Started the American Revolution* (New York: Simon & Schuster, 1988), p. 237.

112 "At most," he writes, "a handful of . . . militia fired at the British": Langguth, p. 240.

112 "four hundred grim farmers armed with muskets": Langguth, p. 244.

112 By day's end, the British had seventy-three soldiers dead: Langguth, p. 250.

114 the scene prompted Daniel Webster: Arthur M. Schlesinger, Jr., *The Age of Jackson* (Boston: Little, Brown, 1945), p. 45.

114 "It was a proud day for the people": *Argus of Western America,* March 18, 1829, quoted in Robert V. Remini, *The Life of Andrew Jackson* (New York: Harper, 1988), p. 181.

116 "shall not have died in vain": Abraham Lincoln, Gettysburg Address, delivered at Gettysburg, Pa., November 19, 1863.

116 "The Almighty has his own purposes": Abraham Lincoln, Second Inaugural Address, March 4, 1865.

117 "the last, best hope of earth": Abraham Lincoln, Second Annual Message to Congress, December 1, 1862.

118 "I felt like the moon": Harry Truman, comments to reporters, mult.

118 "He was not a hero": Mary McGrory, *The Washington Star,* December 27, 1972, quoted in McCullough, p. 989.

119 "I thought two weeks ago": McCullough, p. 204.

120 Truman never did learn how to spell: McCullough, p. 220.

121 "He was the kind of president": McCullough, p. 992.

121 "an object lesson in the vitality": Senator Adlai Stevenson III, quoted in McCullough, p. 992.

122 "America has been very busy": Donald Spoto, *Camerado: Hollywood and the American Man* (New York: New American Library, 1978), p. 1.

Chapter 6. Underdogs

127 All *Rocky* synopsis and dialogue: *Rocky.* Director John G. Avild-sen. Performers Sylvester Stallone, Talia Shire, Burt Young, Carl Weathers, and Burgess Meredith. United Artists, 1976.

127 had submitted thirty-two scripts to Hollywood producers: Tim Dirks, review of *Rocky* (1976), from Greatest Films website, www.filmsite.org.

129 "when they're cheering for Rocky, they're cheering for them-selves": Sylvester Stallone, from Daniel J. Leab, "The Blue Collar Ethnic in Bicentennial America: Rocky (1976)," *American History/American Film* (New York: Continuum, 1988), John O'-Connor and Martin A. Jackson, eds., p. 269.

130 "public sentiment was for Liston": George Plimpton, "Muhammad Ali," *Life,* from *Time* online.

130 "I don't have to be what you want me to be": Muhammad Ali, from Plimpton.

130 "I ain't got no quarrel with them Vietcong": Muhammad Ali, mult.

131 "Man, the USA is the best country in the world": Muhammad Ali, quoted in *Time,* March 21, 1963.

132 All *When We Were Kings* commentary: *When We Were Kings.* Director Leon Gast, Gramercy Pictures, 1996.

133 "a solitary routine filled with daily farm chores": George Mair, *Oprah Winfrey: The Real Story* (New York: Birch Lane Press, 1994), p. 10.

135 "The reason I communicate with all these people": Oprah Winfrey to Mike Wallace on *60 Minutes,* CBS News, December 14, 1986, as quoted in Mair, p. 100.

136 "What I'm trying to do with the show": Oprah Winfrey to Larry King on *Larry King Live,* CNN, September 4, 2001.

136 "Like many, many memorable guests before him": David Skinner, "Matters of the Heart," *Salon.com,* September 20, 2000.

Chapter 7. The Lone Hero

140 All *The Searchers* synopsis and dialogue: *The Searchers.* Director John Ford. Performers John Wayne, Jeffrey Hunter, and Vera Miles. Warner Brothers, 1956.

141 His relentless pursuit: Garry Wills gives an insightful analysis in his chapter "The Fury of Ethan," from *John Wayne's America* (New York: Simon & Schuster), pp. 251–61.

143 "God made us all, white, black and red": James Fenimore Cooper, *The Deerslayer,* quoted in McNulty, p. 49.

144 "For whatever traits the Western Hero is admired": Warren S. Walker, "Buckskin West: Leatherstocking at High Noon," *New York Folklore Quarterly,* June 24, 1968, p. 102.

145 "Hawkeye's frontier spirit, his love of the wilderness": Martin Barker and Roger Sabin, *The Lasting of the Mohicans: History of an American Myth* (Jackson, Miss.: University Press of Mississippi, 1997), p. 5.

145 Cooper admitted: Marshall W. Fishwick, "Daniel Boone and the Pattern of the Western Hero," *The Filson Club History Quarterly,* April 27, 1953, p. 128.

145 Boone background: Fishwick, pp. 122–3.

146 the Easterner was a "dude": Wills, p. 311.

147 "This perennial rebirth": Frederick Jackson Turner, "The Signif-

icance of the Frontier in American History," 1893, *The Frontier in American History* (New York: Holt, 1920), pp. 2–3.

147 "The frontier is the line": Turner, pp. 3–4.

148 "new order" where "immigrants were Americanized": Turner, p. 18.

148 "Steadily the frontier of settlement": Turner, p. 35.

149 All *Taxi Driver* synopsis and dialogue: *Taxi Driver.* Director Martin Scorsese. Performers Robert De Niro, Cybill Shepherd, and Jodie Foster. Columbia Pictures, 1976.

151 All *Shane* synopsis and dialogue: *Shane.* Director George Stevens. Performers Alan Ladd, Jean Arthur, Van Heflin, Brandon de Wilde, and Jack Palance. Paramount Pictures, 1953.

Chapter 8. Pioneers

157 "What do you say? Let's try it!": Charles Lindbergh, from A. Scott Berg, *Lindbergh* (New York: G.P. Putnam's Sons, 1998), p. 115.

157 "Today some would say": Address of Senator John F. Kennedy accepting the Democratic party nomination for the presidency of the United States, Memorial Coliseum, Los Angeles, July 15, 1960.

158 "get this country moving again": John F. Kennedy, fourth televised 1960 presidential debate, transcript from the John F. Kennedy Library, available online.

158 "It was too crowded": Marshall W. Fishwick, "Daniel Boone and the Pattern of the Western Hero," *The Filson Club History Quarterly,* April 27, 1953, p. 123.

159 "I reckon I got to light out for the territory ahead of the rest":

Mark Twain (Samuel Langhorne Clemens), *The Adventures of Huckleberry Finn* (Racine, Wis.: Whitman Publishing Company, 1940).

159 "With his native capacity": Fishwick, p. 124.

159 "Possessing a body": William Carlos Williams, quoted in Fishwick, p. 137.

160 "Western democracy has been": Frederick Jackson Turner, "The Significance of the Frontier in American History," 1893, *The Frontier in American History* (New York: Holt, 1920), p. 261.

162 "He is no longer permitted": *The New Republic,* quoted in John W. Ward, "The Meaning of Lindbergh's Flight," John W. Ward, *American Quarterly* 10:1 (Spring 1958), p. 6.

162 "Captain Lindbergh personifies": Theodore Roosevelt, quoted in Ward, p. 9.

162 "Charles Lindbergh is the heir": *Outlook* magazine, quoted in Ward, p. 9.

162 "I don't think I got": James Stewart, quoted in Berg, p. 121.

163 Account of Lindbergh's flight: based on Leonard Mosley, *Lindbergh: A Biography* (New York: Doubleday, 1976), pp. 101–12.

163 Three hours later: Mosley, p. 107.

163 "To plunge into these mountains": Mosley, p. 107.

164 "To millions of simple people": Mosley, p. 104.

166 "Where am I?": Mary S. Lovell, *The Sound of Wings: The Life of Amelia Earhart* (New York: St. Martin's Press, 1989), pp. 183–84.

166 "So I accept these awards": Amelia Earhart, acceptance speech for Outstanding American Woman of the Year Award, October 1932, as reported in the *Philadelphia Inquirer,* October 6, 1932, p. 1; quoted in Lovell, p. 195.

166 "Aviation had come close to me": Amelia Earhart, *20 hrs. 40 min.; Our Flight in the Friendship* (Putnam, 1928).

167 "At no time during the flight": Amelia Earhart, "My Flight from Hawaii," *National Geographic* magazine, May 1935.

168 "*Why* are you attempting": Earhart, *Last Flight,* p. 55, quoted in Donald M. Goldstein and Katherine V. Dillon, *Amelia* (Brasseys, Inc., 1997), p. 167.

168 "An eerie, intermittent croak": "Soviet Satellite Sends U.S. Into a Tizzy," *Life* magazine 43:16, October 14, 1957.

169 "Artificial satellites will pave": Christopher J. Matthews, *Kennedy & Nixon: The Rivalry that Shaped Postwar America* (New York: Simon & Schuster, 1996), p. 121.

170 "I believe that this nation": President Kennedy, Special Message to the Congress on Urgent National Needs, May 25, 1961.

170 "But why, some say, the Moon?": President Kennedy, Speech at Rice University, Houston, Tex., September 12, 1962.

172 "For the families of the seven": President Reagan, speech on the *Challenger* disaster, Oval Office of the White House, January 28, 1986.

Chapter 9. Optimism

177 Happy days are here again: Jack Yellen, lyrics; Milton Ager, music, 1929.

178 "and about noon had two bills presented to me": George Washington, *The Diaries of George Washington* 6, July 12, 1790, Donald Jackson and Dorothy Twohig, eds. (Charlottesville, Va.: University Press of Virginia, 1979), p. 94, from the George Washington Papers at the Library of Congress, 1741–1799.

178 "Philadelphia stood upon an area of three by two miles": George
    Washington, letter to the Washington, D.C. commissioners, from
    the George Washington Papers at the Library of Congress,
    1741–1799.

179 "No nation perhaps had ever before the opportunity": Pierre
    L'Enfant, letter to President Washington, 1789, from Richard W.
    Stephenson, *A Plan Whol[l]y New: Pierre Charles L'Enfant's
    Plan of the City of Washington* (Washington: Library of Con-
    gress, 1993), p. 13.

179 "proportioned to the Greatnes which a City the Capitale of a
    powerful Empire": Pierre L'Enfant to President Washington,
    from Stephenson, p. 22.

179 "Whilst the Commissioners were engaged": George Washington,
    The Diaries of George Washington 6, June 28, 1791, Jackson and
    Twohig, p. 164, from the George Washington Papers at the Li-
    brary of Congress, 1741–1799.

180 "to fear is fear itself": Franklin Delano Roosevelt, First Inaugural
    Address, March 4, 1933, from The Library of Congress, tran-
    scription from *The Avalon Project* at Yale Law School, available
    online.

180 "On the farms, in the large metropolitan areas": Franklin Delano
    Roosevelt, Democratic National Convention, Chicago, Ill., July
    2, 1932.

181 "I pledge you, I pledge myself, to a new deal for the American
    people": Franklin Delano Roosevelt, Democratic National Con-
    vention, Chicago, Ill., July 2, 1932.

181 "Out of every crisis, every tribulation": Franklin Delano Roosevelt,
    Democratic National Convention, Chicago, Ill., July 2, 1932.

227

182 "It is not enough to clothe and feed the body of this Nation": Franklin Delano Roosevelt, Third Inaugural Address, January 20, 1941, from The Library of Congress, transcription from *The Avalon Project* at Yale Law School, available online.

182 "like opening your first bottle of champagne": Winston Churchill, from James C. Hume, *Churchill* (New York: Stein and Day Publishers, 1980), p. 267.

183 "In the future days which we seek to make secure": Franklin Delano Roosevelt, Four Freedoms Speech to Congress, January 6, 1941.

183 "I have always believed that this land was placed here": Ronald Reagan, the Anderson-Reagan presidential debate, September 21, 1980, transcription from the Commission on Presidential Debates, available online.

186 "I hope you're a Republican" and "Honey, I forgot to duck": Ronald Reagan, mult.

186 "The grace and humor Reagan showed after the attempt to assassinate him": Garry Wills, *Reagan's America: Innocents at Home* (Garden City, N.Y.: Doubleday, 1987).

187 "November 5, 1994/My Fellow Americans": Ronald Reagan, letter announcing he has Alzheimer's disease, the Ronald Reagan Presidential Library, available online.

188 "He would look at the spirit and sacrifice of the firefighters": George W. Bush, at the United States Capitol ceremony honoring President and Mrs. Reagan with the Congressional Gold Medal, May 16, 2002, transcription from the White House Office of the Press Secretary.

189 All *Yanks* synopsis and dialogue: *Yanks*. Director John

Schlesinger. Performers Richard Gere, Vanessa Redgrave, William Devane, and Lisa Eichorn. Universal Pictures, 1979.

190 "Don't talk to me about war" and story about Michael V. Forrestal's meeting with FDR: the source is Timothy Dickinson, friend of the late Michael Forrestal.

Chapter 10. American Exceptionalism

193 "Let us reject the blinders of isolationism": George W. Bush, "A Distinctly American Isolationism," speech given at the Ronald Reagan Presidential Library, Simi Valley, Ca., November 19, 1999.

194 "Now the only way": John Winthrop, "Modell of Christian Charity," sermon for the Massachusetts Bay Colony, 1630.

195 "We have every opportunity": Thomas Paine, *Rights of Man, Common Sense, and Other Political Writings* (Oxford: Oxford University Press, 1995).

196 "the only nation in the world": Gilbert K. Chesterton, quoted in Frederick Edwards, "The Religious Character of American Patriotism," *The Humanist* magazine, November/December 1987, pp. 20–24.

196 "I never doubted": Benjamin Franklin, *The Autobiography of Benjamin Franklin & Selections from His Other Writings* (New York: Modern Library, 2001).

197 "represents Franklin's life as enacting": Deborah L. Madsen, *American Exceptionalism* (Edinburgh: Edinburgh University Press, 1999), pp. 36–37.

197 "poverty and obscurity": Franklin.

198 "There were the Puritans who hated": Robert Ingersoll, Centennial Oration, July 4, 1876, from *The Works of Robert G. Ingersoll,* Dresden Memorial Edition, Vol. IX (New York: The Ingersoll League, 1939), cited in Edwards, p. 36.

198 "We wonder how such saints can sing": Frederick Douglass, *Narrative of the Life of Frederick Douglass, An American Slave,* Christopher Bigsby, ed. (London: J. M. Dent, 1992), p. 573. Cited in Madsen, pp. 88–89.

200 "the last, best hope of earth": Abraham Lincoln, Second Annual Message to Congress, December 1, 1862.

200 "It may seem strange that any man should dare": Abraham Lincoln, Second Inaugural Address, March 4, 1865.

200 "a moral issue . . . as old as the Scriptures": John F. Kennedy, Radio and Television Report to the American People on Civil Rights, June 11, 1963, transcription obtained from the John F. Kennedy Library, available online.

201 "Today we are committed to a worldwide struggle": John F. Kennedy, radio and television report to the American people on civil rights.

201 "This will be the day": Martin Luther King, "I Have a Dream," August 28, 1963, Washington, D.C.

ILLUSTRATION CREDITS

Scribner/Simon & Schuster, and the Rare Books Division, Department of Rare Books and Special Collections, Princeton University Library for the cover of the first edition of *The Great Gatsby* by F. Scott Fitzgerald, page 10.

The Everett Collection and Paramount Pictures for the photo of Cary Grant and Grace Kelly, page 21.

The Kobal Collection and Columbia Pictures for an image from the movie *Mr. Smith Goes to Washington,* page 30.

The John McCain for President Exploratory Committee for the photo of Senator John McCain, page 49.

Cleveland State University and Warner Brothers Studios for an image from the movie *Casablanca,* page 56.

National Archives and Records Administration/Images of American Political History Online Collection, page 60.

Corbis and Robert Maass for the photo of Colin Powell, page 70.

Cleveland State University for the photo of Ernest Hemingway, page 80.

Corbis and The Bettmann Archive for a reproduction of *Washington Crossing the Delaware,* page 91.

The Everett Collection for the photo of Theodore Roosevelt, page 98.

The Kobal Collection and United Artists for an image from the movie *Dave,* page 108.

Corbis for a reproduction of a drawing of Andrew Jackson's inauguration festivities, page 114.

Corbis and The Bettmann Archive for the photograph of Harry Truman, page 118.

The Kobal Collection and United Artists for an image from the movie *Rocky,* page 126.

Corbis and The Bettmann Archive for the photo of Muhammad Ali and George Foreman, page 131.

The Everett Collection for the photo of Oprah Winfrey, page 134.

Corbis and Underwood & Underwood for the photo of John Wayne, page 138.

Print Collection, Miriam and Ira D. Wallach Division of Art, Prints and Photographs, the New York Public Library, Astor, Lenox and Tilden Foundations for the reproduction of the engraving *The Waylaid Travelers* by James David Smillie, from *The Last of the Mohicans* by James Fenimore Cooper, page 144.

The Kobal Collection and Columbia Pictures for an image from the movie *Taxi Driver,* page 150.

Corbis for a reproduction of a drawing of Daniel Boone, page 156.

Cleveland State University for the photo of Charles Lindbergh, page 161.

Corbis and The Bettmann Archive for the photo of Amelia Earhart, page 165.

Cleveland State University for the photo of Franklin Delano Roosevelt, page 176.

The Everett Collection for the photo of Ronald Reagan, page 184.

The Everett Collection and Universal Pictures for an image from the movie *Yanks,* page 190.

Corbis for the photo of Abraham Lincoln, page 192.

Corbis and The Bettmann Archive for the photo of Frederick Douglass, page 199.

Corbis and the Hulton-Deutsch Collection for the photo of Martin Luther King, Jr., page 202.

Index

About the Author

Chris Matthews is anchor of MSNBC's *Hardball* and star of the NBC-syndicated *The Chris Matthews Show.* A veteran of fifteen years with the *San Francisco Examiner* and *Chronicle,* he was a speechwriter for President Jimmy Carter and senior aide to Thomas P. "Tip" O'Neill, Jr., the U.S. Speaker of the House. Matthews is the *New York Times* bestselling author of *Now, Let Me Tell You What I Really Think,* as well as the classics *Hardball* and *Kennedy & Nixon.* Matthews lives with his wife, Kathleen Matthews, news anchor for the ABC affiliate in Washington, D.C., and their three children in Chevy Chase, Maryland.

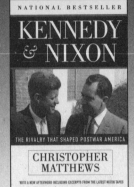